REVIEWS

The Power of Prophetic Parenting is a beautifully written book that provides loving encouragement and guidance to parents through powerful insights from Biblical Scripture. Crissina D. Johnson, an extraordinary African American Mom, shares her journey of raising her children with the guidance of God's Holy Spirit. She emphasizes how this approach led to their personal and professional successes, strong faith in God, loving marriages, and parenthood. Johnson's book helps parents facing challenges discover the clear help that Scripture offers for parenting and nurturing their children's personal growth and God-given gifts. You will find joy in reading this book, appreciating Johnson's splendid writing, and the wonderful discoveries she shares, all by God's grace. It will inspire you to parent prophetically for God's glory. Hallelujah!

—Dr. Oscar Owens, Jr.
Director of Christian Education and Bible College President,
West Angeles Church of God in Christ,
Los Angeles, California

The Power of Prophetic Parenting explores the author, Crissina D. Johnson's life as a single parent and devoted Christian. In it, she talks about her day-to-day interactions with her own four children and the techniques she employed over her forty years of experience as a mother, parent, and prayer warrior who never wavered, surrendered, or stopped believing. Her strength, courage, and tenacity enthralled me, as it will you. I also like how she highlights traditional parenting styles examined through the eyes of clinical and behavior psychologists. Crissina asserts that it is never too late to practice the prophetic parenting methods: communicating with your children through God, prayer, reflection, and meditation. This book is a MUST read for parents wanting to take a leading role in their families' active lives. Crissina shares her extraordinary results using the Prophetic Parenting approach, citing ample examples throughout the book.

—Dr. Anita Barner
Barner & Associates Educational Consultants
Los Angeles, California

THE POWER OF PROPHETIC PARENTING

Practical Tools and Strategies
for Parents to Partner with God
in Raising Children

CRISSINA D. JOHNSON

KP PUBLISHING COMPANY

Copyright 2024 by Crissina D. Johnson

The Power of Prophetic Parenting

All rights reserved. In accordance with the U.S. Copyright Act of 1976, the scanning, uploading, and electronic sharing of any part of this book without the permission of the publisher is unlawful piracy and theft of the author's intellectual property. If you would like to use material from this book (other than for review purposes), prior written permission must be obtained by contacting the publisher at info@kp-pub.com.

Thank you for your support of the author's rights.

ISBN: 978-0-976729-31-0 (Paperback)
ISBN: 978-0-976729-33-4 (Ebook)
Library of Congress Control Number: 2023917725

Editor: Marlaina Ashford-Gordon, KP Publishing Editorial Services
Cover Design: Juan Roberts, Creative Lunacy
Literary Director: Sandra Slayton James

Bible Permissions:
"Scripture quotations taken from the Amplified® Bible (AMP), Copyright © 2015 by The Lockman Foundation. Used by permission. lockman.org"

"Scripture quotations are from the ESV® Bible (The Holy Bible, English Standard Version®), Copyright © 2001 by Crossway, a publishing ministry of Good News Publishers. Used by permission. All rights reserved."

Scriptures marked ISV are taken from the INTERNATIONAL STANDARD VERSION (ISV): Scripture taken from INTERNATIONAL STANDARD VERSION, copyright© 1996-2008 by the ISV Foundation. All rights reserved internationally.

Scripture taken from THE MESSAGE: THE BIBLE IN CONTEMPORARY ENGLISH, copyright©1993, 1994, 1995, 1996, 2000, 2001, 2002. Used by permission of NavPress Publishing Group.

"Scripture quotations marked TPT are from The Passion Translation®. Copyright © 2017, 2018, 2020 by Passion & Fire Ministries, Inc. Used by permission. All rights reserved. ThePassionTranslation.com."

KP Publishing Company
Publisher of Fiction, Nonfiction & Children's Books
www.kp-pub.com

Printed in the United States of America

DEDICATION

This book, *The Power of Prophet Parenting*, is dedicated with immeasurable love and gratitude to my beloved mother, my four children, their wives, and my eight grandchildren:

In Loving Memory of My Mother,
Evangelist, Mother Viola Hamilton

Throughout my childhood, you were a guiding light, and your unwavering dedication to parenthood was truly exceptional. After years of believing you were incapable of bearing a child, your resolute determination and sheer belief led to the conception of your one and only child—me.

From my earliest memories, you instilled in me the values and skills of effective parenting, nurturing my understanding and passion for this vital role. Your persistence, passion, and unique perspective on parenting are etched deep within my soul. Being presumed barren, understanding the crucial role of parenting became of utmost significance to you. Always yearning for the opportunity to become a parent so you could employ all the techniques you believed to be the gold standard for parenting. As I embarked on my journey of parenthood, I often reflected on the parenting gems you'd embedded in me down through the years. It was the fervor, focus, and unwavering commitment you demonstrated that helped to guide my path. Your teachings became the cornerstone of my approach to raising my own children and ultimately inspired the creation of the prophetic parenting style.

I am forever indebted to you, Mom, for the invaluable lessons you imparted. Your memory lives on through this book, and your wisdom continues to illuminate my path. Though you are no longer with us, your legacy is imprinted on every page. Your passionate lessons are eternal and your love remains in my heart.

To My Sons and Daughter

You have been the greatest gifts in my life, bringing boundless joy and purpose. As I crafted the prophetic parenting approach, I drew from the deep reservoirs of the memories and experiences of your childhoods. You were the ones directly influenced by the concepts and ideas that have shaped our family's journey. Stephen, Roman, Marcus and Zion, your unwavering support, endless love, and patient understanding have been my pillars of strength.

Even in moments of imperfection, you saw my genuine intentions—the profound love I hold for you and the spiritual calling that steered my actions. I firmly believe that destiny chose you to be my children, and I treasure your unconditional love and steadfast encouragement you have shared with me for over four decades.

With this book, I aim to honor the unique bond we share and the remarkable individuals you have become. May these pages reflect the

Dedication

warmth of our connection and the invaluable lessons I have learned from each of you.

For the Generations Yet Unseen

This book is dedicated to my eight grandchildren and the countless generations to come. Above all others, you have been the inspiration for me writing this book. To leave a legacy of the values and guiding principles that mean the most to me and our family, in hopes that you will one day embrace them and pass them on to your children's children.

Yeshua, Sophia, Joaquin, Christian, Noah, Ezra, Levi, and Amaya, know that with every word penned, you were in my heart and on my mind. As I navigated writing the pages of this book, it was your faces that appeared before my eyes, embodying the future, full of promise and possessing the potential to carry this work forward.

This book is not just a collection of words; it's a testament to the love, hope, and aspirations I hold for all of you and the generations that will follow. May these pages carry the essence of our family's values, inspiring you to embrace your heritage and to pass down the wisdom of your ancestors for generations to come.

FOREWORD

DR. WANDA DAVIS

(The following words were spoken by Dr. Wanda Davis and recorded on DVD at the inaugural Prophetic Parenting Conference where author Crissina Johnson presented and hosted in 2006. Dr. Wanda's nurturing and powerfully prophetic words spoken have sustained and fueled Crissina to stay on this mission and to publish the book, The Power of Prophetic Parenting.)

IN LOVING MEMORY OF DR. WANDA DAVIS

We just recently reactivated Calling First Ladies, which is national and international organization. And I am going to make sure we utilize you so that we can see and hear the gifts that you have. You have something to say, and you have taken the time to know the word, and to share it, and I want God to give you some opportunities. So, let's stay in touch, because I want to make sure of that.

Sometimes it takes one place to go, and then you're gone! That's all it takes, is one person. Because God used that little crazy tape, Sex Traps to send me all over the world. And that tape is old, and it is still the best seller for Destiny. In fact, last week I was at a Singles Conference in College Park, Georgia and they said, "Would you please tell your publisher to put it on DVD."

God will take the foolish things to confound the wise. I've gotten off planes in other countries, and they've come running up, saying, "You're the sex lady." And I say, "Hey shut up! Somebody's going to get it twisted" (Laughter). But God used that so I could minister other things. And I am going to ask God to open doors for what you're doing. This whole conference needs thousands of people hearing it. And I am so glad they are videoing, and I'm sure they got everything you said. I want a copy of it. I want the Bishop Eddie Longs, and the TD Jakes, and Creflo Dollars, and the Andrew Merits, and the Leroy Baileys, and the Fernandes,' and people who have connections to hear what God has burdened and given you.

See, you have a vision, but visions are birthed out of burdens. And God has burdened, you to know that if we don't start raising our seed righteously, we are not going to have a seed to raise. My mom and dad have 13 of us and none of us are in prison, we are all serving God.

I salute you and I thank God for your vision. I declare that it shall prosper! In the name of Jesus. And the latter days of this conference will be better than the former days. Don't stop! Bishop Jakes told me something one night in the middle of him ministering to about 60,000. He stopped his message and said, "Wanda, remember, my ministry to the women started with 22 people in a Sunday school class." And he went right back into his message. It was as though nobody else heard. Do not despise small beginnings [Crissina]. You just get ready, honey! God's gonna grow this! And you'll be attacked, but you already got the victory. You know that! Because the anointing attracts attacks. So, just get ready. Take your spiritual vitamins, and get ready to fight, because you're doing something that is going to be such a blessing to so many men and women in the kingdom.

> *"Father, we just thank You for Pastor Crissina. We thank You for this vision to challenge and confront us to raise our seed in righteousness. We praise You for this glorious opportunity. Father I'm speaking to thousands of people in this room right now, because I'm speaking to every woman here and every person that is connected to her. And God that means this voice is being heard in so many homes. We thank You for this great opportunity, Father, I know I'm not supposed to be nowhere but right here right now. I give You the glory and the honor in Jesus name! Amen."*

INTRODUCTION

In the 1960s, through Dr. Diane Baumrind, three prominent parenting styles emerged on the scene. Authoritarian parenting, Authoritative parenting, and Permissive parenting. Since then, dozens of parenting styles have been identified. Among them, the most popular are: Helicopter parenting, Gentle parenting, Neglectful parenting, Tiger parenting, Free Range parenting, Authoritarian parenting, Authoritative parenting, Attachment parenting, Spiral parenting, Calm parenting, and Conscious parenting.

Parenting and the style of parenting is of great importance as parents directly impact society and future civilization through the methods they use to parent their children. In this book, I explore the various styles of parenting and put forward a style that, based on my experience, will prove to be the single most supreme, highly effective pattern and style to achieve extraordinary outcomes. I wrote *The Power of Prophetic Parenting* to dispel the myth that children do not come with an instruction manual, as you will discover, in fact indeed they do.

Prophetic Parenting is the style of parenting I created and used within my own home, raising my four children, and as an educator with my students over the last four decades that has yielded remarkable results.

It is with tremendous humility and gratitude that I pen this book. I am humbled and honored to share my parenting journey with each reader. I understand that my words and the concepts revealed within these pages will impact multiple thousands of households across the globe. It is not lost on me the great responsibility I bear to craft my words in such a way as to honor the trust that this assignment places on me.

My journey as a parent began a little over forty years ago, in the fall of 1981, with the birth of my son, Stephen, who possessed an air of royalty. He was calm, observant, mild-mannered, and astute. My second son, Roman has always been very charismatic. He added an element of adventure and spontaneity to our family. The youngest of my three older children is Marcus. Early on, Marcus was a gentle giant. Eleven years after the birth of my youngest son, in 1998, I was blessed with the birth of my youngest child and only daughter, Zion, who was and is the embodiment of God's favor and faithfulness to His promises. It is so incredible how unique and distinct each child can differ from their siblings.

As is the case with most parents, my children were my world, and I could hardly wait to afford them every opportunity imaginable. My children and I would enjoy an incredibly close, loving, tight-knit relationship. They would know they were loved and supported unconditionally. I dreamed of them all being college-educated, accomplished musicians, athletes, incredibly intelligent, articulate,

Introduction

and well-behaved. I desired nothing but the best for them, and with my guidance and presence in their lives, there would be nothing they would not be able to accomplish. But would my love and sheer determination be enough? In a perfect world, possibly this would have been enough. But we do not live in a perfect world. It did not take long for me to recognize I would need to be far more intentional and strategic in my approach to parenting if I wanted to achieve my desired outcomes.

In early 1990, one evening after leaving work and picking the kids up from school, I went grocery shopping at a local market. The boys and I pulled into the parking lot, I parked, we got out of the car, and entered the store. After grabbing a basket and putting my youngest son in the shopping cart seat, I had an epiphany. At that moment, it was as though time stood still, and I was suspended in it. Every fiber of my being instantly stood at attention. Next, I heard the words, **"They will grow up to be who you raise them to be."** I stood there, frozen. I starred at the three of them as though I was seeing them, truly seeing them for the very first time. In that instant, I felt the weight and gravity of my responsibility in a way I had not felt previously. I alone was being held responsible for how my children turned out as adults.

It would be my parenting style that would shape them. It would be my parenting style that would set the trajectory for their lives. God arrested my attention that night, and a few weeks later, in a similar manner, again I heard a very specific set of instructions. **"Your job is to make sure they understand and know My kingdom and how it works. The enemy will make sure they are exposed to the darkness that is of this world."**

The first encounter would ignite a fervor and focus within my mind that would inform and shape the way I would choose to parent my children during one of the deadliest decades in history, especially for African American males. The second laid out my posture and position as their parent. I would stand as the primary presence shielding them from the imminent dangers of a deteriorating culture that would be relentless in its efforts to influence and shape their upbringing.

My duty would revolve around arming them with the knowledge, understanding, and skills to traverse and conquer the harsh, deadly, unforgiving terrain, fostering discernment, self-assurance, and spiritual and psychological resolve, enabling them to opt for the path illuminated by godliness while distinguishing it from contrasting influences. This would mean war. I would need to become a larger-than-life influence in the lives of my children by physically, mentally, and spiritually garbing myself in battle attire and create an environment where they would be exposed to opportunities beyond the environment that surrounded them.

My charge as their parent was to equip them with the boldness, confidence, and self-worth they would need to triumph over every obstacle that would inevitably oppose them and scale or blast through every wall that would seek to contain them. This responsibility was mine alone. Fully embracing my role as their parent, being methodical, consistent, and intentional would become my greatest and most effective attributes.

I became mission-minded, and parenting effectively became my number one priority. Not only would the outcomes of my children be impacted, but I understood my family line and legacy would forever be affected for generations to come as a result of my taking on this herculean challenge.

I began making moves in the spiritual and supernatural realms through prayer, prophetic insight, and employing prophetic strategies and tactical maneuvers. The realm of the prophetic gives you sharp

Introduction

keys and tools to out-strategize the enemy. It would be the only way to achieve the goals I'd envisioned. I deeply understood the power of divine intervention. Second, in importance to me, nurturing the children and developing an authentic, relevant relationship with God (the God of the Bible), I was also intentional about creating an environment of hope and showing them attainable opportunities and paths beyond what they might realize. So, I also ensured they attended the best schools and seized the best options without respect for what society dictated. This pattern became my MO or modus operandi.

My children are the product of a style of parenting that is not new within many communities but one whose time has come to the fore and that I have spent the last forty years refining and will be detailed in this book. Never before has this unique style of parenting been articulated in a comprehensive parenting book or parenting manual, until now. My parenting journey and unparalleled style of parenting demonstrates that in the face of seemingly insurmountable barriers and obstacles, highly effective parenting has and indeed continues to yield extraordinary results.

More than likely, you have picked up *The Power of Prophetic Parenting*, because you are possibly a birth parent, grandparent, or caregiver, and you not only love your children, but you also desire to provide them with the best possible advantages in life. You are proactive and committed to self-development and to discovering ways to improve your effectiveness. You may be a Godparent, a stepparent, a foster parent, an adoptive parent, a teacher, or a youth-worker who desires to positively impact and influence the lives of the children who have been placed in your care. You may have questions regarding the best parenting methods to use. You may be reading this book for insight into how you can provide your children with a healthy balance of nurturance, discipline, restriction, and leniency.

Prophetic Parenting is a rich, dynamic, robust style that fully engages parents and equips their children to produce high moral, social, spiritual, behavioral, and academic success. It is a style and approach to parenting that would provide me with my desired outcomes despite of my background and family history. This book will help you form highly effective strategies and give you clarity and direction making your parenting journey manageable and rewarding. *The Power of Prophetic Parenting* is divided into four, easy-to-read sections.

The first section investigates the components of traditional parenting styles providing insight into the purpose and effects of these styles according to clinical and behavioral psychologists. You will be able to develop a working knowledge of various styles of parenting and identify which styles most closely resemble your own. This section will also stretch and challenge you to identify areas where it may be necessary for you to adjust your current approach to parenting.

The second section walks parents through the essential fundamentals of basic parenting based on my forty years of parenting expertise. In this section, the reader will discover timeless tools, techniques, and strategies I incorporated into my day-to-day interactions with my children.

The third section goes beyond the basic essentials and details the essentials of Prophetic Parenting and how parenting from an elevated place of awareness, spiritual connectivity, and accountability has the potential to dramatically enhance your parenting outcomes. You will find these parenting essentials to contain the nuts and bolts of parenting that you have been seeking.

The fourth and final section, 'Nuances and Nuggets of Effective Parenting' provides the network of connective tissue that will hold your entire prophetic parenting experience together. This final section

Introduction

deep dives into the various nuances associated with prophetic parenting and provides the reassurance that you are still on the right track even in times when it may seem everything you are striving to accomplish is falling apart.

What makes *The Power of Prophetic Parenting* a must-read is my personal story of resilience and success in the face of insurmountable odds. I attribute 100% of my success as a parent to this style of parenting. Prophetic Parenting not only saved the lives of my children from being capsized and utterly destroyed by the culture or peer pressure, but this parenting style is also responsible for creating new norms and waves of generational blessings that will reverberate throughout my bloodline for generations to come and it will do the same for you.

Take a moment to release yourself from the stress and pressure of not being good enough as a parent. Perfect parents do not exist. There are no perfect parents just as there are no perfect children. I sense there are many reading this book who are at a loss, not knowing what to do or how to best parent the child(ren) God has blessed your life with. You have bought into the notion that no "guidebook" for parenting has been written. It often makes you feel lost, overwhelmed, uncertain, or ineffective. I have been directed to pen my experiences as a parent in hopes that something that is shared within these pages will provide you with the support and reassurance, insight, understanding, and the path forward you so desperately desire.

The Prophetic Parenting style leans into scripture, not religiously or for formality, but wholly and completely leaning in, identifying, and extracting morsels and nuggets of truth, insight and instruction understanding that God Himself is a faithful father who provides everything His children need to succeed in every area of their lives, including parenting. What you will discover housed within several biblical passages are practical, applicable guiding principles that will play a huge role in guiding and directing you through your prophetic parenting journey. Woven within, there are various biblical passages sited, you will uncover practical and applicable guiding principles. These principles will significantly contribute to guiding and directing you along your Prophetic Parenting journey.

Like many of you, when I embarked on this journey, I had very little to go on. My children were being raised in a day and time that was much different than how things had been when I was a child. I needed help, and I was not afraid nor ashamed to seek it. It is said necessity is the mother of invention. Prophetic Parenting is the style of parenting I developed and refined over the years out of my own deep, desperate desire to provide my children with an edge and an advantage in life that would rival the advantages afforded their peers who had access and exposure to far more resources and opportunities than my children had.

From the onset, I had no interest in my children falling prey to the culture, being ordinary or barely scraping by in life. Raising them to one day becoming extraordinary individuals was my goal from the onset. Prophetic Parenting afforded me the ability to design a style of parenting that embraced the wisdom of my faith, my ancestors, my culture, and my community while incorporating real-time revelation knowledge, prophetic strategies, original concepts, and relevant techniques that would be useful to any parent in any environment or dispensation of time.

Prophetic Parenting enlists and instills a kingdom perspective and a biblical worldview rooted in the tenets of the Christian faith. A strong emphasis is placed on biblical accounts, God's love, His care, concern, and His plan for each parent and for each child. Parents access details and information regarding God's specific plan for their

Introduction

child's life through communication with God via prayer, reflection, meditation and observation. Each parent's relationship and experience with God is going to be unique and distinct and may present a little differently from household to household. It is expected.

The primary objective is for parents to acknowledge that God has a purpose and plan for their child that He is willing to reveal, and well able to provide guidance and assistance along the parenting journey. Not every parent who embarks on the journey of Prophetic Parenting will have the gift of prophecy or be called to the office of a prophet, but what every parent does have is the word of God [Bible]. You may or may not be dealt with regarding your children through dreams or visions or words of knowledge or words of wisdom, but if you have the holy scriptures, you can read and speak the word of God over your children's lives. Scripture is just as powerful when it is read, spoken, and declared as it is when it is divinely revealed and inspired.

Proverbs 29:18 is your lighthouse passage. This passage of scripture will stand tall, towering far above the chaos and uncertainty that you will inevitably encounter as a parent. Proverbs 29:18 will illuminate your path and provide a beacon of light when dense fog clouds your judgment, and it feels you have lost your way. It will faithfully navigate you back to your mission and purpose as a parent.

> *"When there is no clear prophetic vision,*
> *people quickly wander astray.*
> *But when you follow the revelation of the Word,*
> *heaven's bliss fills your soul."* (TPT)

There's a remarkable and almost magical transformation that occurs when a child is nurtured with a deep sense of belonging to a grander purpose. Such a child approaches life's challenges with remarkable self-awareness and a clear sense of direction. They naturally conduct themselves with honor and confidence. A beautiful outcome of this Prophetic Parenting approach is that your child becomes a trusted source of wisdom and guidance, looked to by their peers and admired by adults.

It is a testament to the profound influence of Prophetic Parenting. Depending on your child's personality, you might witness this transformation in their early years or observe it unfolding as they mature into their teenage and young adult years. In either case, the impact will be unmistakable.

CONTENTS

Dedication   *vii*
Foreword   *xi*
Introduction   *xv*

CHAPTER 1:	The Backdrop	1
CHAPTER 2:	Parenting by the Pattern	11
CHAPTER 3:	Parenting with Power	23
CHAPTER 4:	Parenting with Style	33
CHAPTER 5:	Mindset Matters	45
CHAPTER 6:	Peeling Back the Layers	57
CHAPTER 7:	From Tots to Teens	73
CHAPTER 8:	A Snapshot of Parenting Within the African American Community	85
CHAPTER 9:	Training Wills	99
CHAPTER 10:	They're Just Kids!	1
CHAPTER 11:	Dismantling Generational Curses	127

CHAPTER 12:	Legacy Unleashed: Ready, Aim, Fire!	135
CHAPTER 13:	Eshet Manoah	139
CHAPTER 14:	Where Are They Today?	147

Acknowledgments — *157*
About the Author — *159*
References — *161*

CHAPTER 1
THE BACKDROP

To every dynamic, captivating story, there is an equally informative, dynamic backstory. Here's mine, or at least a portion of it. For a fuller, deeper understanding, like many of you, I am the person who digs deeper to understand the context and conditions surrounding a particular matter. Before delving into the transformative insights presented in this impactful book, I feel it is essential to grant you a glimpse into the environment that shaped my parenting journey and the development of Prophetic Parenting.

The 1980s was an incredibly eventful decade with significant technological, political, and economic shifts along with major medical advances. The Space Shuttle lifted off in 1981, and the Berlin Wall fell in 1989. The IBM personal computer is released, the AIDS Epidemic became recognized, and Global Warming became well known. The 80s were riddled with wars as well, Afghanistan, Iraq, the Lebanon war, and the First Intifada in the Gaza Strip and the

THE POWER OF PROPHETIC PARENTING

West Bank. Islamism became a powerful, political force in the 1980's giving way too many terrorist organizations sprouting up. "Gene Therapy," "Designer Babies," and gestational surrogacy all made their first appearances in the 80's. The creation of the internet, video games, and music videos were also introduced to our global community. Michael Jackson became a global icon. Whitney Houston, Duran Duran, and Madonna soared to popularity as well. My children were being born at a time when the world was changing dramatically and I would need to prepare them not only to survive but to thrive in this new, ever-changing world.

My older three children were born in the 1980s, which, as mentioned above, was indeed an incredibly eventful decade globally. Closer to home, however, in the greater Los Angeles area, we were excited and proud that the 80's brought the 1984 Summer Olympics to our backyard. Of all the advances of the 80's, it would be the crack cocaine and gang epidemics that thundered into our community like the waves of a deadly tsunami that would have the most profound impact on the day to day lives of the families, businesses, and neighborhoods across the United States and even more so in large, inner city communities like Los Angeles.

Almost overnight, friends, neighbors, and family members, young, and old were becoming addicted to crack. Those who were not using crack were dealing it. Unlike cocaine with its high end, affluent crowd of users and dealers, crack addicts were not hidden behind the doors of 5th Avenue corporate boardrooms or the walls of upscale, posh country clubs or million-dollar estates. Crack cocaine was not hidden at all. Its effects poured out into the streets seeping into every nook and cranny of society and life. Its horrors played out in plain view, in back alleys, at gas stations, on school campuses, in church sanctuaries and on street corners. Families of all socioeconomic statuses were hit hard. Mothers, fathers, grandparents, doctors, nurses, preachers, and teachers were becoming addicted to crack, signing over the deeds to their homes, their churches, and the titles to their cars, selling their jewelry, television sets and even selling their own children in exchange for the smallest morsel of crack cocaine. It became common place seeing teen girls and grandmothers alike degrading themselves, selling their bodies and exchanging sexual acts for crack.

Out of the crack explosion arose the birth of crack babies—babies whose mothers were addicted to crack causing them to be born with neurological and psychological maladies, being sensitive to touch, inconsolable and often shaking uncontrollably. As these crack babies grew older, medical professionals and behavioral psychologists found these children to often be without a conscience, indiscriminately brutal to others, often having behavioral challenges, lacking judgment or the ability to feel remorse, to care or have compassion for others. In pre-school, middle school, high school, and college, these affected children would be my children's peers.

During the 1980's crack epidemic, family homes were either being lost to dope dealers or being converted to "crack houses." Crack houses, sprinkled far and wide, were establishments where crack cocaine was manufactured and processed 24 hours a day, seven days a week. A place where dealers and addicts sold and used crack around the clock. Manufacturing crack cocaine was considerably inexpensive causing the sale of crack to turn extremely high profits. Before long, teens and even younger children were being recruited to sell crack. Those who did, easily turned an astronomical profit often earning more money than doctors, lawyers, or corporate CEOs. Raking in quick cash, in many instances upwards of five and six figures monthly became a significant part of the culture, notably among pre-teens and teens. Because of this dynamic alone, there was a remarkable shift of power affecting the parent-child relationship. In many cases, even parents with the best intentions weakened their stance against drugs and began relying on the economic stability the drug money their children were earning provided. These youth became the providers for their families, shouldering the responsibility of keeping a roof over the family's head, paying rent, car notes, utilities, buying groceries, and purchasing school clothes for their siblings. There was a shift in power. Roles were reversed and the parent's authority often, undermined.

As a young, single mom, I'd done a pretty decent job during the 80's shielding my little ones from many of the harsh realities and effects of the crack epidemic. I kept them involved in sports and enrolled them in the Royal Rangers, which was a faith-based version of the Boy Scouts. We attended church together where they sung in the choir, participated in weekly Sunday School classes, Christmas plays, and Resurrection Day recitals. On some weekends, I would load their bikes onto the back of my Jeep and drive out to Shoreline Village to enjoy cycling and looking at the Spruce Goose. I set a high standard for academic achievement and did everything within my ability to teach them to be respectful, well-mannered, caring, and considerate. I had a vision for my children that did not include them falling prey to the streets. I did everything within my ability to create a safe, loving, supportive environment with high standards and strong expectations. As the 1980s ended and the 90s rolled in, I felt relatively confident that my parenting style would continue to produce my desired results. By the mid to late 1990s, my older two sons had reached their teens and my youngest son was not too far behind. They were doing well academically and athletically. I'd landed a promotion at my job which enabled me to purchase my first home in an older, well established, upper-middle class neighborhood—a comfortable distance from the crack induced depravity playing out on the streets of other neighborhoods. Life was good. I was defying the odds, protecting my children, and providing a comfortable lifestyle for myself and my children. There appeared to be minimal threat to them becoming successful, productive, contributing members of society. Gradually, however, there began to be an uptick in what I initially thought were random acts of violence tied to the crack world. I could not have been more wrong.

In 1993, murders reached their highest point nationwide. Gradually, I remember hearing more and more about instances of drive by shootings and gun-related murders. At first, these were news stories of events happening in places far enough away from my neck of the woods that I still had a sense of safety. As the months rolled on, reports of the violence intensified. Each instance seemed to grow closer and closer to home Soon I realized that the violence I thought was crack-related was actually gang-related. The 90's brought an astronomical surge in the prominence and dominance of violent street gangs. Gangs had always been in existence, but this was different. Remember those kids who had been recruited to sell crack? Well, along with selling crack came the threat of being robbed or murdered, so there grew an overwhelming need for protection. The environment was ripe for the formulation of a perfect storm. The gang element was already in place with their system of territorial control. Crack dealers could use the protection their neighborhood gang could provide. These two power brokers merged their objectives, and the violence played out in city streets everywhere. Soon, neighborhoods, churches, and schools were being overtaken by gangs. Stories of children being violently assaulted by gangs spread like wildfire. Gang members were killing one another in broad open daylight.

My children were now at an age when they were most susceptible to being impressed by the culture and their peers. Much to the dismay and consternation of countless parents, the teen years are when many parents report they lose their children to outside forces. To make things worse, a large number of these street gang members were school-aged children! Children who were the same age as my own children. I witnessed one parent after another suffer the loss of their child. Drive-by-shootings had become a significant part of everyday life. Parents were petrified that their son or daughter would be the next victim. Young teens were being "put on" or "jumped into" gangs at record rates. The hearts of parents and families were being ripped apart and thoroughly devastated as their sons were being murdered in the streets. When I spoke to other parents, there was an overwhelming sense of helplessness. Parents were desperate and were frantically doing everything within their power to save their children and get them as far away as possible from the impact and influence of these violent gangs.

I remember an article in one of the local newspapers showing a picture of a wall that had been "tagged" with graffiti that read "Rolling 60's Crips"—the name of a gang in the Los Angeles area. What made the article so profound was that the photograph had been taken in a small town, down south in Alabama. A frustrated resident was quoted in the article telling the California gang members to "go back where they'd come from," an emphatic statement that their brand of violence and behavior were not welcomed there. Parents were frantic and desperate. Children were being shipped out of state to family members, and other families were fleeing the violence and carnage of Los Angeles was moving to less populated areas of neighboring counties. The moves were being made in hopes of escaping the horrors and carnage of gang violence and of saving the lives of their sons and daughters.

What many of these well-meaning parents were unaware of was that frequently, the children they'd shipped off or loaded in the back of the station wagon were already gang-affiliated, and deeply entrenched in the gang-crack culture. These moves to new locations merely served to further spread the presence and influence of gangs to new territories and there was no escaping it.

Countless times throughout my parenting journey, I would be complemented as having done an incredible job as a parent. Especially as a single parent raising sons in the inner cities of Southern California. But my response would consistently illuminate my belief that God had blessed me with absolutely incredible children. However, as true as that may be, and as effective as I may have been as a parent, today, I recognize that the outcomes I achieved are 100% attributed to the power of prophetic parenting!

Like every other child that has ever been born, my children are imperfect humans, not gods. They are flawed and have their weaknesses and imperfections just like anyone else. However, who they are and what they have become are overcomers. Individuals who are not swayed by what is going on in culture or influenced by their peers. Individuals who possess a keen sense of self, are self-confident, self-motivated, humble, teachable, and purpose-driven. Each of them overcame the worst of the 1980s, 90s and 2000s with their lives, their freedom, and their God-given identities intact. They are examples to their peers, and to parents everywhere that prophetic parenting has an overwhelming effect on the outcomes of children. This book details a style of parenting I have spent the last forty years refining, but is not new within many communities and my children are a direct result.

Never before has this unique style of parenting been articulated in a comprehensive parenting book or parenting manual, until now. My parenting journey and unparalleled style of parenting demonstrates that in the face of seemingly insurmountable barriers and obstacles, highly effective parenting has and indeed continues to yield extraordinary results.

Parenting in the 21st century comes with a whole new set of concerns and challenges. The escalating occurrences of school shootings, human-trafficking, adolescent homicide, and suicide have left us deeply troubled. Moreover, our children are constantly exposed to godless doctrines and belief systems that work tirelessly to deceive and sway them from their values.

The influence of parents, preachers, and Sunday school teachers has been overshadowed by the pervasive presence of the internet and social media. As a result, the glamorization of violence through video games, drug use, self-indulgence, and lawlessness has eroded the cherished values society once held dear. Consequently, we find ourselves facing a generation of enraged, isolated, and confused minors, often struggling with clinical depression.

Our children are under siege, and it is natural for us, as caring individuals, to seek the best possible outcomes for them. To not only shield them from harm, but to also position them for massive success. However, navigating this daunting task in today's culture can be overwhelming, leaving us uncertain about the most effective approaches to protect and guide our children.

If *The Power of Prophetic Parenting* has grabbed your attention and you have decided to purchase it, it is because you are a devoted parent or caregiver, deeply invested in the well-being of your children. You have decided to become a part of a larger community of parents who are just as conscientious and committed as you are! Your proactive nature and commitment to self-improvement drive you to seek ways to enhance your parenting skills.

The Backdrop

You might be grappling with questions about the most effective parenting approaches. Your reason for delving into this book could be to gain insights on providing your children with a balanced blend of nurturing, discipline, boundaries, and flexibility. Whatever motivated you to choose this book, it will also guide you through a transformative journey, helping you become a highly effective and influential figure in the lives of your cherished children.

CHAPTER 2
PARENTING BY THE PATTERN

When The Pattern Is Right, The Glory Will Fall." Several years ago, a local minister preached a compelling message based on the building of the temple in Jerusalem found in I Kings 4–8; I Chronicles 28 and II Chronicles 3 and 4. By revelation knowledge, God had given King David the specific instruction on how the temple was to be constructed, furnished, and decorated. The height, breadth, length, and depth of the temple were specific to the smallest measurement. It included every conceivable detail including the dimensions of all the rooms and their furnishings, the weight of the gold and what was to be solid gold or gold overlay, the colors and fabrics to be used for the curtains and priests garments, the weight of the candlesticks, the weight of the lamps, the table of shewbread, the flesh hooks, the bowls, the brazen altar, the Holy of Holies, the two pillars, the porch, the brazen altar the golden lamp stands and the courts and doors. Every aspect of the temple was constructed in accordance with what God had instructed. And in the ninth chapter of I Kings, after Solomon followed God's pattern and completed the construction of the temple; in verse 3 the Lord says,

> *"I have heard your prayer and your supplication, that you have made before Me. I have hallowed this house, which you have built, to put My name there, forever and My eyes, and my heart shall be there perpetually."* (KJV)

Solomon followed the pattern and the glory (presence) of God filled in the temple. This is what I needed! I desperately needed the glory of God to fall on me, the parent and I longed for God's eye and His heart to be with my children perpetually. I knew that, short of an act of God and divine intervention, my children would likely be consumed by the culture that surrounded them. I needed to discover what God's pattern for parenting was and once discovered, I needed to be found following it with all my heart and soul as Solomon had when constructing the temple. Understanding that without His guidance and instruction, my efforts would be futile.

It would take a power beyond my own to intervene and divinely accomplish what could never be accomplished in my own strength. But what does a parent do when they do not know where to start? One of the most challenging positions for a parent to find themselves in is to have a sense of what they desire for the lives of their children but need a guide or any guidance on how to accomplish their desired outcomes. This position is where I found myself. When I started my parenting journey, I was full of passion and determination to achieve certain specific outcomes. I had a clear idea, and I was driven by this purpose, yet I lacked the blueprint. I had never seen done what I was hoping to accomplish. What I envisioned creating with my children had been birthed in my heart, and I could see it in my mind's eye but I had no practical step-by-step plan. When I looked at the parents around me, honestly, I did not see the type of results I had any interest in duplicating. Somehow I sensed that there was a way of parenting that was far more dynamic and effective than anything I'd experienced or witnessed up until that time. I was being drawn to dig deeper, to search further and press beyond the typical religious traditions and practices many parents ascribed to that just were not yielding high results. To achieve the results I desired, my approach to parenting would require me to apply the full weight of God's word and His way of doing things to my parenting practices.

Within the book of Deuteronomy, I found what I had been looking for. A simple, yet powerful guideline or pattern for raising children. As a child, I remember being fascinated reading the various accounts in the book of Deuteronomy as God led his holy people, Israel, from Egyptian captivity into the land of promise. I recall being absolutely enamored with the continued instruction, encouragement, warnings and admonishments God spoke to Israel and over the years, would reference Deuteronomy whenever I needed reminding of God's faithfulness and the benefits of being obedient to His word. Especially eye opening were the blessings God would pronounce on Israel as a result of their continued obedience and the consequences or curses that would befall Israel should they rebel against God's word or His way of doing things. I'd read through the book of Deuteronomy a dozen times over the years, but it was not until I was searching for a parenting manual did I see that God's pattern for parenting had been right there in the book of Deuteronomy all along!

After years of hearing it said that "children do not come with instructions" or "there is no parenting manual on how to raise children," I found myself adopting that erroneous philosophy. But something in my mind kept moving me towards scripture. I could not reconcile what I knew and believed about God being a provider, and a supplier of every need with Him not providing or supplying an instructional guide for parents on how to parent effectively. It just did not add up. There had to be something, somewhere, in the scriptures that equipped parents to parent effectively, and here it was, right here in the book of Deuteronomy!

As a parent, I recognized early on the grave responsibility that had been placed on my shoulders to raise my children to a higher standard. The evening that I heard God speak to me that my children would become the adults that I raised them to be stayed with me every moment of the day and night. The account in Deuteronomy really resonated with me. Like Moses, I felt that I was being charged as a parent to teach my children, lead them, encourage them, and keep them in remembrance of God's goodness, His faithfulness and His mighty acts. I also felt, like Moses, to warn my children and admonish them not to fall prey to the enemy's schemes to diminish and destroy them and prevent them from entering into the life of provision, abundance, good health, prosperity, and wealth God has purposed for them. The day I heard God speak to me about my responsibility to raise them effectively was when I believed I was being called to develop and design a robust style of parenting that I and countless other parents could use to achieve extraordinary results with their children. I was being divinely called to lead my children into their land of promise as are you.

In Deuteronomy, God lays out an instructional guide on how families were to conduct and govern themselves once they entered the land of promise, including guidelines on how to raise their children, what their diet was to be and how they were to worship if they desired to be blessed, thrive, prosper, and continue in their land of promise.

As a single parent, living in an urban, metropolitan area, where my children's peers were gang-banging and murdering one another in the streets, I was determined to find and follow a parenting strategy that worked. I took every instruction and direction of Deuteronomy to heart. Contained within this one book, I found the tools, techniques, and methods I sought. They were right there, hidden in plain view. So, I applied them. Little by little until the patterns and processes of Deuteronomy became the culture and environment in which my children would be raised. As a parent, I always envisioned my children as being the ones who would shatter norms and break barriers. I always saw the greatness of God in them and felt it was my duty to raise them in such a way that they were cognizant of their God given purpose, and fully equipped to thrive and excel in their respective areas of influence.

The book of Deuteronomy picks up with the previous generation having been disqualified from entering into the Promised Land. Now God's fulfillment of promise was left to the next generation to carry the mantle and cross over out of wandering into promise. One of the first exercises Moses had the children of Israel do was to look back. Look back and to remember. Not only to remember the faithful miracles of God, but also the rebellion and disobedience of the previous generation. Taking a long, honest look at how far God had brought them was critical for their future success. Just as critical was their recognizing, acknowledging, and owning the errors and disobedience that was a significant part of their history. The children of Israel needed to be clear that how the previous generation had dealt with God cost them the opportunity to go forward. This exercise also helped fuel Israel's commitment to adhering to God's way of doing things. They were moving into something new and God did not want them to fall prey to their old ways of thinking and being. This passage of scripture spoke volumes to me as a parent who was being charged to chart a new path for my children. It was important for me to acknowledge and embrace all the blessings and achievements of my ancestors while also acknowledging the areas where they fell short. Like Moses, I kept my children in remembrance of both. God's power, His faithfulness, His promises, and the ramifications associated with deviating from His plan.

A significant aspect of my parenting strategy was to be as transparent, open, and honest with my children as possible regarding my failures, shortcomings, and ignorance. I also determined to alert them to the generational default settings that had ambushed me and many of my close relatives. To excel, one must not live in the past but must take a hard, honest look at the past to fuel forward momentum and not repeat past mistakes. Even Moses had been forbidden from entering the Promised Land, Joshua would be the one chosen to take the people into their destiny. Parents must be less concerned about presenting a polished, perfect image of themselves as they are giving their children the gift of being able to learn from their failures, not only enjoy successes. Embrace the fact that you are chosen by God, handpicked to raise the children you have been blessed with, flaws and failures and all.

Next, Israel's attention was turned to focus on God, His mighty acts, miraculous deeds, sovereignty, and His matchless power. While wandering through the wilderness, the children of God had an opportunity to see God at His finest. Even before the splitting of the Red Sea, and the crossing over on dry land, there had been plagues and mighty deliverance wrought by the hand of God. While in the wilderness, they were fed supernaturally; manna fell from heaven, they were given water to drink from rocks and even meat to eat when they requested it. Every need had been divinely and supernaturally provided. For the next generation to walk into greater doors of opportunity than the previous, they needed to know that the God of the Bible was with them and was more than capable of providing for their every need. This is the same God my children needed to know. Not only did they need to know Him, but they needed to understand that He knew them even before they were born, and that He was well able to carry them forward in life.

In Deuteronomy 4:9

> *"Only pay attention and watch yourself closely so you do not forget the things which your eyes have seen and t hey do not depart from your heart all the days of your life. Make them known to your children and your grandchildren [impressing these things on their mind and penetrating their heart with these truths.]* (AMP)

What things had this generation seen? They had seen the miracles performed in the wilderness and Moses instructed them to be vigilant and remember and also to make God's mighty acts known to their children and their grandchildren. Parents and grandparents play a tremendous role in shaping the faith of their little ones.

> Deuteronomy 6:6-12 is a little more explicit, *"Write these commandments that I've given you today on your hearts. Get them inside of you and then get them inside your children. Talk about them wherever you are, sitting at home or walking in the street; talk about them from the time you get up in the morning to when you fall into bed at night. Tie them on your hands and foreheads as a reminder; inscribe them on the doorposts of your homes*

and on your city gates. When God, your God, ushers you into the land he promised through your ancestors Abraham, Isaac, and Jacob to give you, you're going to walk into large, bustling cities you didn't build, well-furnished houses you didn't buy, come upon wells you didn't dig, vineyards and olive orchards you didn't plant. When you take it all in and settle down, pleased and content, make sure you don't forget how you got there— God brought you out of slavery in Egypt. (MSG)

There it is! Clearly articulated in scripture! The parenting manual that we so often hear said does not exist. But here it is plainly recorded in scripture. The instructions to parents on how to raise your children. This is what I would do. This is how I would raise my children. This would be the pattern I would follow. I took these words to heart and understood that I was being used to create a new reality for my children that had not previously existed. For all intents and purposes, I was their Joshua, leading the charge and helping them cross the Jordan into their land of promise. There were certain seasons in their lives when I could sense were pivotal, and it felt as though I was on a covert mission smuggling my children from a life of death and destruction to a life of prosperity and abundance. Every instruction that is given here in Deuteronomy to the children of Israel regarding their inheritance, I took and believed and implemented in my conversations and parenting style.

One of the most popular chapters of the entire Bible is the 28th chapter in Deuteronomy. It is here where God uses Moses to detail the blessings of Israel's obedience and the subsequent curses of Israel's disobedience. Verses 1-14 describe the abundant blessings that will befall the obedient. Here is a small sample of the blessings that would overtake Israel for her obedience: Deuteronomy 28:1-7 (NIV),

> *"If you fully obey the Lord your God and carefully follow all his commands I give you today, the Lord your God will set you high above all the nations on earth. All these blessings will come on you and accompany you if you obey the Lord your God: You will be blessed in the city and blessed in the country. The fruit of your womb will be blessed, and the crops of your land and the young of your livestock—the calves of your herds and the lambs of your flocks. Your basket and your kneading trough will be blessed. You will be blessed when you come in and blessed when you go out. The Lord will grant that the enemies who rise up against you will be defeated before you. They will come at you from one direction but flee from you in seven."* (NIV)

Obedience brings benefits.

These were the blessings I earnestly desired the lives of my children to be marked by! I started this journey like most parents do, with a strong desire for my children to reach their highest potential. To be successful and safe. To be conquers and overcomers. I hoped that I could raise them in a way that they would know and understand that God had a divine and unique purpose for their lives-that the path God had purposed for them would look very different from the paths of many of their peers. God has been faithful to His word and to His promises. But that's just it—God is always faithful to His word. So raising children from a word-based perspective fixes the fight and gets as close as humanly possible to guaranteed outcomes. When the pattern is right, the glory will indeed fall.

Parenting according to God's pattern will place you in direct conflict with and in opposition to the culture and the secular world view. I will not mince words or present a diluted, whitewashed version of what it means to raise your children according to God's pattern.

Any time you step into the realm that is governed and ruled by the God of the Bible, the authority of His word and His way of doing things, you are instantaneously placed in a militarized zone. Parenting prophetically places parents in the heat of a spiritual battle over the lives and outcomes of their children. You become a living, breathing intercessor standing in the gap between the kingdom of darkness which seeks to destroy the lives of your children and the kingdom of God, which seeks to preserve your children's lives from destruction. In the middle of these two extremes is where I frequently found myself during my children's formative years, and should you pick the mantle to raise your children according to God's divine pattern, so will you also find yourself opposing and being opposed by the kingdom of darkness.

There were instructions God would give me regarding my children that outside observers just did not understand. One example of this was that I would speak affirmations over my children every morning before school.

These affirmations were largely based on the blessing listed in Deuteronomy 28:1-14. But, I would also add, "You are employers and not employees!" After hearing me speak this over my children's lives a time or two, my mother pulled me to the side one day. Evidently, it had been troubling her that I would speak these words in particular. Her concern was that I was teaching my children not to work or have jobs. I remember her saying, "Crissy, they are going to be men and they have to know that they will need to work and have jobs." My mother had lived through the Great Depression and was a part of a generation where landing a good paying job was the only viable path to achieving the "American Dream." I explained to my mother that I was not teaching my children not to work, but rather, I was creating an environment in their thinking while they were young to open their minds to the reality that they could one day become owners, bosses, and entrepreneurs. My intent and purpose were for this affirmation to ignite a vision within them where they would begin visualizing their future selves as creators, innovators, and possessing the wherewithal to chart their own paths in life. To be the ones providing employment opportunities for others. God had me shaping their mindset to reach higher and not be limited by an "employee" mindset or "slave" mentality. I wanted them to understand that being the boss was attainable. Parenting prophetically produces power. Powerful conversations and encounters as your children begin to see themselves as more than ordinary and experience the divine intervention of God in their lives.

Parenting according to God's pattern may cost you your pride. It may cause you and your parenting techniques to draw criticism or to be misunderstood by well-meaning family members and friends. Your children may not understand the reason you make certain decisions and choices regarding them. No matter how uncomfortable or how ostracized you may feel from time to time, you can rest assured that when parenting according to the pattern set forth in God's word, God has you covered. He is moving on your behalf and in the lives of each of your children. His hand on your children's lives will be conspicuous and undeniable; the favor and blessing they walk in will be unmatched and inexplicable! No other style of parenting can rival prophetic parenting as it acknowledges God's authority, submits to God's sovereignty, welcomes God's intervention, and unleashes God's favor and grace.

CHAPTER 3
PARENTING WITH POWER

What makes parenting prophetically more powerful and effective than parenting based solely on intellect or emotion? Prophetic parenting is backed by the full weight and force of God's foresight, foreknowledge, insight, and presence. It positions parents on the right side or on God's side in every situation that might arise! Prophetic parenting provides the cheat code parents need to navigate effectively through the parenting matrix. Proverbs 3:5-7 says,

> *"Trust God from the bottom of your heart; don't try to figure out everything on your own. Listen for God's voice in everything you do, everywhere you go; He's the one who will keep you on track. Don't assume that you know it all. Run to God! Run from evil! Your body will glow with health, your very bones will vibrate with life!"* (MSG)

This passage reveals yet another pattern that if applied to your approach to parenting, will yield extraordinary results.

There are two key points in this passage that are directly aligned with prophetic parenting. The first "don't try to figure everything out on your own!" Take a moment and understand that, on your parenting journey, God is offering you His presence, His divine intervention and unwavering support. His word will guide you and His spirit will infuse you with supernatural strength, insight, and ability. You are not left to figuring everything out by yourself. The second key prophetic parenting point found in this passage is, "Don't assume that you know it all. Run to God!" The greatest parent of all-time is God Himself. He is our loving, gracious, all knowing, and just Heavenly Father. As informed, well-read and prepared as you may be, parenting prophetically will always lead you to a place of seeking God for His wisdom, His knowledge, and His direction as it pertains to raising the children He has entrusted to your care.

Though life happens and unforeseen situations and circumstances arise, at your fingertips are the solutions and remedies to address every situation. Prophetic parenting is divine and supernatural. With this style of parenting, as a parent, you are never at a loss. You have the assurance that God is moving in the unseen realms working things together for your good and bringing to fruition and into manifestation His perfect and divine will and purpose for your children's lives. Prophetic Parenting is the absolute, most effective parenting method ever developed and there will not be a more effective form of parenting to replace it. Here are the reasons why:

So, what does it mean to be prophetic or to operate in the prophetic? Prophesy is the supernatural ability to accurately describe or predict what has happened in the past and what will happen in the future. Being prophetic describes a person who possesses the ability to see, hear, know, understand, and speak the heart, mind and will of God with the authority granted to them by the Holy Spirit. Signs, wonders and miracles are released into the earth realm through the prophetic by activation and demonstration of a combination of the following spiritual gifts:

The gift of wisdom, the gift of knowledge, the gift of faith, the gift of healing, the gift of miracles, the gift of prophecy, the gift of discernment of spirits, the gift of different/divers kinds of tongues and the gift of interpretation of tongues.

These spiritual gifts are listed and can be found in I Corinthians 12:8-10, 28 (NIV).

These nine spiritual gifts are the equivalent to spiritual power tools. Through these gifts, the full power and authority of the Holy Spirit are imparted to individuals gracing them to execute God's will on earth. Receiving wisdom and knowledge from the heart and mind of God then speaking it, declaring it and decreeing it into existence.

Now, that's power! Of the nine spiritual gifts, the ones I found to be most vital to the Prophetic Parenting style are: **The Word of Wisdom**, **The Word of Knowledge**, **The Gift of Faith**, **The Gift of Prophecy**, and **The Discerning of Spirits**.

The Word of Wisdom is the supernatural ability to know a specific plan-of-action or set of instructions to employ in the midst of a specific set of circumstances. Supernaturally knowing what to do, how and when to do it. The sons of Issachar operated in this supernatural ability. Of the sons of Issachar it is recorded that they were,

"men who understood the times and knew what Israel ought to do." (I Chronicles 12:32)

It is an invaluable benefit to understand the times. Many fail, however, to know what the plan-of-action should be in any given moment of time. Just as futile as knowing the plan-of-action but not knowing the time to execute it. There will be times along your parenting journey when you will need a divinely inspired "word of wisdom (instruction)."

The Word of Knowledge is supernatural and divine knowledge; a download of information and insight that otherwise be hidden or not evident. Words of knowledge are frequently referred to as "a knowing." This gift supernaturally unveils and reveals the truth of a matter through a strong impression or sudden revelation similar to having an "ah-ha" moment often through a dream or a vision. The transmission of this knowledge can transpire at any given moment, day or night through a thought, vision or even a dream.

The Gift of Faith is a divinely inspired belief accompanied by corresponding actions and declarations. These actions and declarations are based on the revelatory gifts of the word of wisdom, a word of knowledge, prophecy or the discerning of spirits. This divinely inspired belief and its corresponding actions are not subject to or limited by what is seen or presumed based on the obvious; nor by the situations or circumstances at hand. A person who operates in the gift of faith will speak and act boldly, without wavering or doubt. Faith is a word that denotes action. The gift of faith is supernatural in that, in the face of insurmountable odds, it creates realities that result from the words and actions of the person graced with this power gift. In Romans 4:17, it is said of God that,

> *"He quickens the dead and calls those things that be not as though they were."*

This passage demonstrates the power of words spoken in faith. Doubtless, parents who are parenting prophetically will find themselves operating in and utilizing this powerful tool while raising their children. Possessing a strong belief that the preordained will and purpose of God for their child's life will come to pass even in the face of opposition and adversity.

The Gift of Prophecy is the supernatural gift to know and to speak the heart and mind of God. It is the single most instrumental gift to have in your utility-belt when raising children. The words spoken from your mouth as their parent, carry tremendous, life-altering weight and have the ability to shape the lives of your children for decades and even generations.

Having the ability to speak directly from the heart of God to your child is invaluable. From a prophetic parenting perspective, the gift of prophecy encapsulates the word of wisdom, the word of knowledge, the gift of faith and even discerning of spirits.

This power tool causes parents to become the conduits through which your children will recognize the importance of knowing God's will for their lives, and begin hearing God's voice, accessing His power, and aligning themselves with His will for themselves.

The Gift of Discerning of Spirits is the supernatural ability to detect and identify spiritual entities. Often referred to as discernment, this power gift enables one to grasp and comprehend that which is obscure or hidden. Having the supernatural ability to peer beyond the superficial. To identify and plainly see ulterior motives and masked ill will. This gift empowers parents to use wisdom, accurately judge individuals and situations that arise in their child's life, and helps parents guide their children to avoid snares, traps, ambushments, and pitfalls designed to seduce and to destroy their child.

THE POWER OF PROPHETIC PARENTING

Prophetic parenting is about creating a prophetic culture around your children, beginning at the early stages of their psychological and spiritual development. It's about training and exposing your child to the world of spiritual gifts and powers available to them through developing an intimate, personal relationship with God and with his word.

Prophetic parents prioritize equipping and empowering their children to know the word of God, seek the will of God and to develop a sensitivity to the voice of God as the means through which they are acutely aware, vigilant, discerning and are able to distinguish between which matters are in alignment with God's purpose and plan for their lives, and which matters are not.

Listen, there is no pressure here. Parents, if you feel at a loss or overwhelmed by the necessity for you to function, flow, and operate in all the spiritual power tools listed above to parent effectively, do not! Remember that greater than all these powerful gifts is love (I Corinthians 13:2). When you approach parenting from a place of genuine, unconditional love as mentioned previously, you will find that your sensitivity to your child's needs, and to God's voice will gradually grow keener. Do not feel pressured to force yourself to function or operate in giftings that you do not believe you possess. This approach would defeat the purpose.

Remember, parenting prophetically is not rooted in religious or hypocritical displays of virtue. But rather, Prophetic Parenting is born out of a pure heart and a sincere desire for God to grace and empower parents to parent effectively, and achieve extraordinary that otherwise would not be attainable. Love first, then the power-tools will follow. I Corinthians 12:30 states that none of us possess all the spiritual gifts: healing, tongues, and the interpretation of tongues. No! But verse 31 goes on to say that we are to earnestly covet or desire the "best" gifts. What are the "best" gifts? The "best" gifts are the ones that are needed to be in operation at any given time. What's the point here? As you parent your children prophetically, acknowledge there are power tools at your disposal endowed with them in the most needed moments.

The Power of Prophetic Parenting begins with you knowing and speaking the written, inerrant, divinely inspired word of God—the Holy Scriptures. You can gain wisdom, knowledge and words of affirmation from scriptures that have already been inspired by God and recorded for your benefit. As a prophetic parent, when you yield to God's word and His way of doing things, you have access to this arsenal of spiritual gifts or "power tools" needed to accomplish your role as a parent with the full weight of God and heaven backing you. Parenting prophetically grants parents access to the fullness and power of God, working through you as a parent to unleash your child's full potential and create an environment where what God has purposed and spoken in His word supersedes and overrides all else. Parents receive new thoughts, fresh ideas, are able to identify and establish new pathways and ways of living through parenting prophetically. When speaking before large arenas filled with parents or conducting one on one coaching and training, I encourage them to view themselves as being the priests, bishops, pastors, evangelists and teachers in the home. One of the most powerful benefits of parenting prophetically is the parent's ability to know and speak God's will and word to their children and over their children's lives bringing into manifestation the fullness of heaven on earth.

It is what I needed and what many of you need as well. I needed the supernatural power and ability to override the reality that my children were being raised by a divorced single mother, in communities that were plagued by poverty, homelessness, drugs and gang violence. I needed the authority and ability to confront, cast down and abolish the pressure and influence of their peers, popular culture, and diabolical societal norms. I needed to strikeout out and overwrite what statistics and the culture predicted about my children with what the word of God had to say about them. Prophetic Parenting transitions a parent from being solely reliant on themselves and their limited abilities and resources to being God reliant or reliant upon God, His power, His word and His unlimited resources in helping to get the job done. Prophetic Parenting provides for the understanding that although there will be real realities parents face with their children in this life, there is another reality that is even more real than the one that can be seen with the natural eye. In the face of the worst, least desirable set of circumstances, God's reality is the only reality that matters. If a parent has the ability to see or to know or understand reality from God's perspective, they are then able to bring God's reality into manifestation in the lives of their children.

As you can see, Prophetic Parenting is a rich, dynamic, robust style of parenting that fully engages parents and equips their children to produce high moral, social, behavioral and academic success.

THE URGENCY OF NOW!

What is it about today that causes Prophetic Parenting to be of such tremendous importance? When my children were little, I understood that the world they would one day live in did not yet exist and that raising them based purely on how the world was in the past or solely on the present would not suffice. They would need to be equipped with coping skills and other intellectual, emotional and spiritual tools that would be relevant decades into the future. Qualities, attributes, strengths and characteristics that were not only typical for today but applicable and useful tomorrow. The tomorrow of yesterday is here today and although I knew the times would be vastly different in the future, I could not have imagined the extent to which children would be under siege as they are in today's world.

Parenting with Power

Children are falling prey to human traffickers, bullies and school shootings. Homicide and suicide, depression and feelings of alienation amongst young children are at an all-time high. Children are increasingly being molested and abused by family members, trusted loved ones, teachers, and even clergy. Alarmingly, these incidents are becoming more common in the lives of one of the most vulnerable populations in our society: our children. Politicians, medical professionals and parents are at a loss as to how to combat this increasing assault against our little ones. Their first line of defense is you! You are the one God has chosen and hand-picked to raise, defend, protect and equip the next generation. All parents have the responsibility to protect and safeguard their children, but prophetic parents also have the ability, power and authority to make a measurable, sustainable and death-defying difference in their children's lives.

Over my nearly sixty years on this earth, I have witnessed parents become overwhelmed with raising their children, have thrown in the towel, grown weary of the fight and ultimately lost control of the entire matter. Do not buy-in to the deception that you are powerless, because you are not. We have arrived at a point in time when children are targeted and bombarded at every conceivable level. The internet, television, video games, music lyrics, music videos, movies, TikTok, IG, Facebook, Twitter reels, shorts and stories and dozens of other social media sites vie for your child's attention; for your child's heart, their affections and their very soul often drowning out the voice and influence of their parents and certainly the voice of God, their creator. I do not want to get ahead of myself, but I will say, today's society is very much like the environment in Babylon under the rule of King Nebuchadnezzar.

Reflecting back, I realize now what at the time I did not fully comprehend. That is, just how monumental of a discovery I had made when beginning to enlist the techniques and strategies of prophetic parenting. Over the next eighteen years, I would lather, rinse and repeat the same prophetic parenting philosophies, tools, strategies and techniques I'd employed the previous twenty-two years.

Raising my sons but now using them with my daughter who faced a new set of enemies that my sons had not. No longer was it the crack epidemic or gang affiliation that plagued our streets and posed the greatest concern. No, through technological advancement, the internet, cell phones and social media platforms, the dogmas and doctrines of the depraved culture had direct access to children. In many instances bypassing the watchful eyes of the most vigilant parents.

Mom, Dad, Godparent, Grandparent; your hands are not tied! This book will help unleash your parenting potential and propel you into an arena where you regain the power to pierce through all the voices, images, apps, tweets, reels, and posts to make significant inroads into your child's hearts and minds.

The tools and techniques, insights and instructions shared within these pages are the same tools revealed to me years ago when my children were young. I knew the day was approaching when it would be necessary for parents to be equipped with a supernatural means of raising their children and the only way to access this supernatural ability would be for parents to turn to God and to His word in ways they may not have ever considered. Parents are our children's superheroes helping them to survive and to thrive in the midst of the worst conceivable realities impacting children today.

It is impossible for me to share every experience and every nugget of wisdom I have gained over the years, it is however, possible to pull the curtains back and share how Prophetic Parenting style can be helpful to you on your parenting journey and empower you to raise your children who possess a strong sense of purpose along with the resolve to not permit the pressures of the culture or their peers to derail them.

CHAPTER 4
PARENTING WITH STYLE

The concept of parenting styles was first introduced by clinical and behavioral psychologist Diane Baumrind in 1960 to explain differences in the way parents attempt to control and socialize their children. Parenting styles have a significant impact on children's psychology. Broadly, behavioral psychologists agree there are a number of unique and distinct parenting styles that have a deep and long-lasting effect on child development, adolescent behavior and overall achievement among other aspects of life.

According to Doctor Baumrind, the purpose of drawing distinctions between parenting styles is to "explain differences in the way parents attempt to control and socialize their children." The objective of the majority of parents is to find the most effective ways or techniques to "control and socialize" their children. Stick a pin here, this information is going to be key as we look deeper into the most effective styles of parenting or the most effective tools, techniques and strategies parents can use to control and socialize their children. There are three main styles of parenting that describe most parents and they are Authoritarian Parenting, Authoritative Parenting and Permissive Parenting. A fourth style was added to this list a few years later, Uninvolved or Neglectful Parenting, in my experience and opinion based on the purpose for having a parenting style, uninvolved parenting is not parenting at all and borders on the parent being non-responsive and negligent, and certainly not invested in controlling or socializing their children. However, you will see this style of parenting emerge later as you continue to read. It may be shocking to find just how many of us have fallen into this neglectful approach to parenting. Pay close attention to each style of parenting, its pros and its cons. Take copious notes and open your mind to examine each parenting style and consider which aspects of each style might benefit you in achieving your goals as a highly effective parent. Allow yourself the freedom and space to reflect, grow and evolve.

AUTHORITARIAN PARENTING:

With the authoritarian parenting style, according to Baumrind, there is an expectation that the child or children will strictly follow the rules and regulations set by the parent. The Baumrind definition of Authoritarian Parenting suggests a rather distant, cold relationship between parent and child. Parents are far more apt to punish their children when the children are disobedient. Authoritarian parents fail to give any explanation or reason for the rules that are imposed by them. If a child asks for an explanation, the simple reply might be, "Because I said so." Usually, these parents are less responsive and have high demands and expectations. According to Baumrind, these parents "are obedience-or status-oriented, and expect their orders to be obeyed without explanation". Such parents expect complete cooperation from their children and are not at all tolerant about the rules and regulations set by them. Authoritarian parents expect maturity on the part of children and are less interactive with their children. Children of such parents are usually focused on their studies and tend to perform well academically. They develop the habit of staying out of trouble, understanding there are consequences for their behavior. In its strictest form, the negative impact of this parenting style is that the children may not be socially developed as they are never motivated or encouraged to give or develop opinions. Children raised by authoritarian parents are often shy, lack confidence and lack decision-making power. This may make them less interactive and negatively affect their decision-making power. One report describes discipline by the authoritarian parent as often being punitive with the parent withholding love or using shame to control their child's behavior.

AUTHORITATIVE PARENTING:
Authoritative parents, on the other hand, aim to strike a balance between being firm but also warm and supportive. Instead of forcing children to follow rules just because, authoritative parents will discuss rules and expectations as a family. Children raised by authoritative parents are still clear on who's in charge. Authoritative parents will hold their child accountable when they do not do what is expected. When discipline is used, it is usually in the form of coaching or guiding natural and logical consequences. Of the parenting styles, experts often considered the authoritative style of parenting as the gold standard or happy medium between the strict authoritarian parenting style and the permissive approach. Authoritative parents do set limits for their children but are also responsive to their children's needs. Consider it a firm but nurturing style. "Parents operate similarly to

CEOs, but in a less rigid way that allows the child to learn from consequences," Schafer says. Authoritative parenting is widely considered to be a healthy approach to parenting. Children of authoritative parents tend to be friendly, socially interactive, confident, cheerful and cooperative, as well as curious, self-reliant and goal-oriented, research shows.

PERMISSIVE PARENTING:
According to the experts, permissive parents are warm and may even be overly nurturing. There is a tendency with permissive parents to be lax (or inconsistent) in the rules and discipline department. These parents usually act more like a friend than a role model, so children tend to have a lot more freedom to do as they please and are not always monitored closely. Children of permissive parents are not held to a higher standard and often lack having any standard at all. The child is allowed the freedom to chart their own path. There is no expectation for the child to be or to become accountable or responsible to anyone other than themselves. With children parented by permissive parents, having respect for or acknowledging anything or anyone outside their own wants, wishes and desires is never required. Children of permissive parents tend to be free thinkers who are not afraid to speak their minds as brashly or disrespectfully as they feel toward any person at any time including their parents. Some experts believe this might mean more creativity, for example, but being raised in a household without many limits can have many downsides, as being told "no" at home is a way for children to adapt to the reality that boundaries exist in every part of their outside world. (WhatToExpect.com) The negative impact of such a parenting style is that the child's emotional development is harmed and damaged. The child does not mature in key areas. Permissive parenting tends to lend itself to one

of two scenarios: "You end up with either a child who's entitled or incredibly anxious because there's no one in charge running the ship," Schafer says.

Walfish paints a bleaker picture of the most lenient of parenting styles. In the worst-case scenario, without boundaries, consequences, realistic expectations or any structure or protocol for appropriate behavior, she says, children being raised by permissive parents tend to:

- Grow up with poor emotion regulation.
- Become rebellious and defiant when they do not get what they want.
- Don't persevere when faced with challenging tasks.
- Engage in antisocial behaviors, like drug and alcohol abuse, vandalism and theft. (Bump.com) (Parenting Styles and their Effect on Children Behavior)

While not one of the original Baumrind parenting styles, Neglectful Parenting was added to the matrix in 1983 by Eleanor Maccoby, a professor of psychology at Stanford University, and her colleague John Martin. Uninvolved or neglectful parents are not able to meet the emotional or physical needs of their children and provide little parental supervision. Their inability may be tied to emotional, mental, physical or psychological deficiencies. In neglectful parenting, parents do not respond to a child's needs or place any demands on their child. These parents are usually less demanding, less communicative and less responsive. They manage to fulfill the basic needs and necessities of their children but overall, they are less attached to their children. In some cases, these parents are either oblivious, indifferent or detached to the extent that they may even ignore the needs and necessities of their children. In its most extreme form, this type of parenting can border on the parent being criminally negligent leading to the authorities getting involved, since being neglected puts children in danger. Although uninvolved parenting can take on many different forms—most of us would recognize it when we see it. Children of such parents develop negative features in their personalities and lack confidence, lack communication, encouragement and praise. They are not socially active nor confident due to less compliance demand by parents which stunts their social growth. Research shows that children of uninvolved parents tend to have low self-esteem, and they frequently have a hard time forming healthy, trusting relationships with others.

Initially, I did not feel it necessary to explore Neglectful Parenting as a parenting style. Being neglectful, as an approach to parenting seemed contradictory. Of all the various styles of parenting, being neglectful or uninvolved, in my opinion, bordered more on a parent possibly having emotional, mental or physical limitations that prevented them from being responsive to their children. My plan was to not address this area at all until, like a title wave, a flood of thoughts overwhelmed my heart and I understood I was being required to give voice to this style of parenting or non-parenting.

Uninvolved or Neglectful Parenting is a style of parenting where parents do not respond to their child's needs beyond the basics of food, clothing and shelter. Neglectful parents are emotionally unavailable and fail to connect with their children on any level. These parents simply could care less what their child is doing, what they are involved in or how they ultimately turn out. An uninvolved parent might frequently be heard saying, "I feed you, clothe you and provide a roof over your head and that is all I am required to do." Of all the various parenting styles discussed herein or not, Neglectful Parenting would be the style of parenting that is the furthest from Prophetic Parenting.

Parenting with Style

Midway through writing and doing rewrites for this book, it occurred to me that there is, however, a group of parents who have determined to be uninvolved and neglectful as it relates to the spiritual growth and development of their children. This parent would not consider themselves to be a neglectful parent—however, from a biblical and prophetic perspective, that is exactly what this parent would be considered.

A neglectful parent is one who would say, "I am just going to let my child figure out their faith on their own." "I am not going to hold my child to any particular stand as it relates to faith or whether they have a relationship with God or not." This parent has chosen to turn a blind eye and a deaf ear to the patterns that are set forth in God's word and in-so-doing are not only rejecting God's way of doing and being as a parent but are also choosing to produce ill-prepared and ill- equipped children. Contrary to biblical standards and principles, this category of neglectful parent so dramatically deviates from scripture and their God-breathed responsibility as a parent to teach and train their children, that their child is left defenseless, ill-equipped, and ill- prepared in the most crucial areas of their psychological and spiritual development. These parents have no vision for the lives of their children or they are naively believe the vision they do possess will somehow organically spring up like a blade of grass through a city sidewalk trampled underfoot and soon fades away shortly after emerging. What a disservice in their parenting duty! These parents have little to no purpose of their own and are unwilling to do the personal development and work needed to discover their own unique purpose and prepare their children to discover and walk in theirs as well.

Woe and warning to the parents who neglect to raise their children in accordance and in alignment with the pattern God has provided.

THE POWER OF PROPHETIC PARENTING

Woe and warning to the parent who names the name of Christ yet fail to do His word regarding their responsibility as parents. Woe and warning to the parents who demand obedience from their children while walking in opposition against God's word themselves. I understand this is a hard word to hear especially within the pages of such an affirming book. However, there are some who are being admonished to step it up, to get back on track, to realign yourselves with the parenting pattern set forth in scripture, and not leave the future of your child to chance. All admonishments are breathed from love. See the love, feel the care and know God loves you and cares for you enough to bring this area to your attention. Yes, parenting is not an easy assignment. Fatigue, frustration and discouragement often set it. But I hear this passage of scripture for you, "Do not be weary in well doing. You will reap, if you do not faint." Get up! Get back in the fight! Engage! Do what you know to do, and if there are areas where you find yourself at a loss, ask for help! Seek wisdom, pray, and refer to the pages in this book to help light your path.

I am very excited about the emergence of a new style of parenting that is making headway in today's culture, Gentle Parenting. Gentle Parenting is also referred to as positive parenting, attachment parenting, or peaceful parenting. Gentle Parenting is an approach to raising children that prioritizes empathy, respect, and understanding. Instead of relying on traditional punitive measures, gentle parenting focuses on building a strong, positive relationship between parents and children. The core philosophy involves treating children as individuals with their own thoughts and feelings, fostering open communication, and guiding them through challenges with patience and positive reinforcement.

Parents practicing gentle parenting avoid harsh punishments and instead seek to understand the underlying reasons for their child's behavior. They emphasize connection over control, acknowledging that children are learning about the world and their emotions. Setting clear boundaries with explanations, active listening, and offering choices are key elements of gentle parenting. The approach encourages parents to view discipline as a teaching opportunity rather than a punitive measure, helping children develop self-regulation and a sense of responsibility.

Gentle parenting also recognizes the importance of parents modeling the behavior they wish to see in their children. This is key, key, key and also a significant component of Prophetic Parenting. By providing a nurturing and supportive environment, parents aim to foster their child's self-esteem, emotional intelligence, and overall well-being. The approach is adaptable and encourages parents to consider the unique needs and personalities of their children, promoting a positive and cooperative family dynamic.

Roughly a decade ago when law professor Amy Chua wrote and published: Battle Hymn of the Tiger Mother. Amy is of Chinese descent and wrote the book initially as a memoir and to compare and contrast the parenting methods of Chinese mothers with those of "Western/European" parenting methods. Tiger Parenting refers to a strict, authoritarian method of parenting that is meant to raise high-achieving children. This often means forgoing sleepovers, parties, and other leisurely activities to focus on their studies. Chua speaks about her experience implementing tiger parenting methods with her own daughters and her eventual transformation as a mother following her daughter's rebellion. Chua's book was the first of its kind and brought tiger parenting strategies to light in the mainstream media.

What causes so many to be interested in dissecting this particular parenting style are the extraordinary outcomes experienced by an astounding number of Chinese children. "Chinese Americans are over-represented in many of the nation's elite universities" notes Yong Zhao and Wei Qiu. Chinese children get higher SAT math scores, and are disproportionately represented among U.S. National Merit Scholars (Zhao and Qiu 2009). Contrary to popular belief, these outcomes are achieved not because Chinese people enjoy an innate advantage in IQ, because they don't. When James Flynn analyzed past studies of achievement and IQ, he found that Chinese students' attainments could be better explained by environmental factors (Flynn 1991). So, what's the secret?

Yale law professor Amy Chua says it's all about parenting. Chinese mothers raise more accomplished, academically successful children because they are more demanding and stricter than Western/European mothers are according to Professor Chua. Parents who practice Tiger Parenting methods believe strict parenting methods benefit children by setting them up to succeed in the future. In addition, adults who use tiger parenting strategies feel that by setting a high bar, they are instilling a strong work ethic in their children. This approach, in turn, ideally encourages self-discipline that often carries over into adulthood.

Children raised under Tiger Parenting methods are taught to become accustomed to working hard from an early age. While Chua described Tiger Parenting in her book as purely power-assertive, studies show there is room for positive parenting strategies among many people who practice tiger parenting. This includes being warm and supportive as opposed to being exclusively strict.

In some communities here in the heavily European influenced Western world, authoritarian parenting causes children to feel distant and detached from their parents. As though their parents do not love or care for them because they are being strict. Conversely, in other populations, children are far more apt to interpret the authoritarian approach as a sign that their parents love and care for them deeply. Something similar may apply to traditional Chinese families. Psychologist Ruth Chao has proposed a cultural variant of authoritarian parenting, chiao shun, which she translates as "training." According to Chao, chiao shun emphasizes harmonious family relationships—not the domination of the child. The full definition of ciao shun is teaching and training children in the appropriate or expected behaviors or morals. For instance, Chua says she never allowed her kids to have a playdate, watch TV, participate in a school play, or choose their own extra-curricular activities. The kids are also not allowed to "get any grade less than an "A" or "not be the No. 1 student in every subject except gym and drama."

When her seven-year-old daughter failed to master a new piece on the piano, Chua drove her relentlessly. "I threatened her with no lunch, no dinner, no Christmas or Hanukkah presents," Chua writes, "no birthday parties for two, three, four years." When she still kept playing it wrong, I told her she was purposely working herself into a frenzy because she was secretly afraid she couldn't do it. I told her to stop being lazy, cowardly, self-indulgent and pathetic. Chua made her daughter work into the night, denying her even a break to go to the bathroom. "The house became a war zone, and I lost my voice yelling, but still there seemed to be only negative progress, and even I began to have doubts." Then, at last, the girl made a breakthrough. She mastered the piece and wanted to play it again and again. And the emotional strife had lifted. That night, the girl crawled into her mother's bed, and they "snuggled and hugged, cracking each other up. "Unlike many Western/European parents who would have backed down, convinced that the child just wasn't ready or capable of mastering the new piano piece, Chua believed that her child could do it. But she would not learn the piece without intense effort, and that effort was not going to happen unless the child was pushed.

"The Chinese believe that the best way to protect their children is by preparing them for the future, letting them see what they're capable of, and arming them with skills, work habits and inner confidence that no one can ever take away."

Understanding these styles of parenting will aid you in identifying and designing the style that you believe will be most effective for you and your child and most in alignment with the outcomes you desire to achieve.

CHAPTER 5
MINDSET MATTERS

Before diving too deeply into the basic fundamentals of effective parenting and unpacking the effect your style of parenting will have on your children, I would like to take a moment to first speak to the mindset needed before embarking on your parenting journey. All sustainable success begins with an individual first establishing the proper set of perspectives, attitudes, beliefs and thoughts or mindset. Every encounter you have with your child will reflect your state of mind in that moment. So, here are a few perspectives that heavily influenced my approach to parenting and my interaction with my children that I hope will:

MINDSET MATTERS 1:
PARENTS ARE GOD'S CHOICE:
Whether you are a biological parent, step, foster, adoptive or Godparent, you have been chosen to make a significant difference in

the life of the child that is in your care. Your presence in the lives of your children is not a mistake or coincidence. You have been divinely chosen to occupy your position as a parent and as a result, no one else can do the job quite like you can. Because you have been chosen for this assignment, you do possess the capacity and ability to be effective. The fact you are here, reading this material indicates just how conscientious, self-aware and committed you are to the process. It is completely normal to experience feelings of inadequacy along the way, but faithfully remind yourself that you are God's choice and every resource, tool and even the wisdom and support you need will without doubt come to you.

MINDSET MATTERS 2:
CHILDREN ARE GOD'S GIFT:

"Don't you see that children are God's best gift?

The fruit of the womb His generous legacy?"
Psalm 127:3 (MSG)

The Message Bible states in Psalms 127:3 that *"children are God's best gift."* God's best gift? If you have been a parent for any length of time, you might agree that not every moment as a parents feels as though your precious little one is "God's best gift." In fact, there are times when being a parent can be overwhelming and raising your child can be far more challenging than rewarding. Let's be real, there may even be a time or two when you have felt your child was more of a burden or an inconvenience than a gift. Some parents prepare years in advance for the arrival of their children having every provision pre-planned and in place before their arrival. In other cases, the birth of a child is unexpected or inconvenient and no preparations have been made to welcome them into the world. Wherever you find yourself as a parent, remind yourself that you are God's choice and your child is God's best gift. Regardless of the circumstances surrounding their arrival, only the best is in store for you and for your little one. You will be stretched and even stressed beyond anything you could have imagined prior to becoming a parent. As you continue to learn and grow as a person and as a parent, you will gradually discover just how much of a blessing your little one is now and will turn out to be.

There is quite a bit of talk these days about legacy and leaving a legacy for the next generation. This Psalm asserts that "the fruit of the womb [children] are His [God's] legacy." What exactly does this mean? In what ways are children God's legacy? Webster's Dictionary defines "legacy" as "something transmitted by or received from an ancestor or predecessor or from the past." According to Becki Andrus, "a legacy captures your life and the lessons learned along the way, or it celebrates things that were most important to you, such as a cause or an interest. Having a lasting legacy means that you share these deeper meanings with friends, family, and posterity." Children, as God's legacy, are purposed to capture, transmit and celebrate the things that are the most important to God. Children are God's best gift.

MINDSET MATTERS 3:
LOVE RELENTLESSLY AND WITHOUT CONDITION:

Decisively, unconditional love is the most crucial component of parenting. Love without conditions, obligation or fear is the glue that will support, bind and connect all other aspects of your parenting experience together. Unconditional love is not a feeling or an emotion. To love without condition is a decision. It is an attitude and a mindset. Feelings change and emotions fluctuate depending on the circumstances, but making the decision to love without condition must become a consistent constant within your household. Constructing an environment where your children understand and know that your motives and movements are guided by the unconditional love you have for them, provides your children with a sense of security and understanding there is and will always be a trustworthy, reliable, safe place found when they think of you. Let's not get it twisted, as a parent you will be tested and challenged, stretched and possibly even stressed by your children. You will have your share of disagreements and battles. Issues will arise and will fall. Conflicts will come and they will go. Make the decision today to never allow the words that come out of your mouth, your reactions, behaviors or demeanor cause your child to question or doubt the love you have for them. Consistently demonstrating and expressing unconditional love for your children will leave an indelible imprint, overshadowing every hurt or challenge that would ever attempt to convince them otherwise.

Love is a strong, resilient force that takes on many forms and is expressed in various ways. According to I Corinthians 13:4-8 (NIV),

"Love is patient, love is kind. It does not envy, it does not boast, it is not proud.
It does not dishonor others, it is not self-seeking, it is not easily angered, it keeps no record of wrongs. Love does not delight in evil but rejoices in the truth.
It always protects, always trusts, always hopes, always preserves. Love never fails." Hebrews 12:6, 11 (NIV)

Love is not always soft, accommodating, passive or permissive as some parents might presume. On the contrary. Love is bold, strong, confrontational and selfless. Love speaks the truth and is firm and tough as well as tender. Parents who make the decision to love their children without condition sign up for robust relationship with their children without favoritism or partiality. Allowing the full nature, essence and expressions of love to take the lead. Such parents are able to strike a balance between both the stern and the genial aspects of love.

Find the priceless parenting nugget tucked within Hebrews 12:5-11 on the love-discipline dynamic. This dynamic challenges parents to not fall prey to a mindset that says coddling and indulgences are the prevailing indicators of love. They are not. Discipline, direction and training are equally, if not more vital expressions of unconditional love.

For the Lord disciplines the one he loves . . .
No discipline seems pleasant at the time, but painful.
Later on, however, for those who have been trained by it,
it produces a harvest of righteousness and peace.

MINDSET MATTERS 4:
PURPOSE DRIVEN AND MISSION MINDED:

Of the billions of sperm that were feverishly endeavoring to fertilize the one egg of your mother's womb, you are the product of the one sperm that beat out all the others. Therefore, you are not a mistake, nor an accident. Your life began as being the one who prevailed. The one who won! The one who was purposed to be here and the same is true for each one of your children. In the early 1990's, I was introduced to the teachings of Dr. Myles Monroe who described purpose as "knowing and understanding what you were born to accomplish." Dr. Monroe confronted the mediocrity of a generation with thought provoking statements that challenged individuals to know the reason they had been given life and to live their lives in passionate pursuit of their purpose. Such statements include:

- "The greatest tragedy in life is not death, but a life without a purpose."
- "It is better to be dead and not have to worry about living than to live and not know why."
- "Until the question 'why' is answered, there can never be fulfillment."
- "When purpose is not known, abuse is inevitable."
- "Do you know why you are here?"

This message of purpose was so profound, it left an indelible mark on my life and radically transformed the way I thought about myself and the way I began viewing my children. As a parent, my thoughts shifted from not only seeking to discover the purpose for which I was born, but to also discover the purposes for which each of my children had been given life. My mindset changed. My newly discovered mission as a parent was to instill in my children that they each had been uniquely designed for a specific, God-breathed purpose and to equip and empower them to discover their purpose and then passionately pursue it.

This one shift in my mindset set our family on a course that has forever changed the trajectory of our lives. My life as a parent and their lives as children and now as purpose driven adults. As I witnessed the powerful impact the message of purpose was having on my own children, I knew it was a message that would be equally as effective with other parents and children.

In the late 1990's, I owned and operated a home-school co-op/private Christian, K–12, school. Students of all ages received a Christian education and were taught many of the same principles I am sharing here in this book. One of the homework assignments I tasked my middle school and high school students with was to go home and pray; ask God to reveal to them what His purpose was for their life both spiritually and in the secular arena.

We had been studying how many young people in scripture had been chosen and used mightily by God to affect their culture. So, their assignment was to identify in which ways they believed God desired to use their lives to impact today's culture. Each student had exactly one week to complete the assignment and return to class with what they had discovered about themselves and about God's plan for their lives. "God has called me to be a psalmist and a child psychologist" is what I remember one student sharing with the class. They each understood their assignment and came back with incredible insight into the path they believed God had ordained for them. I wanted to awaken this part of their understanding and make them cognizant of the fact that they could know with certainty who they had been purposed to be or become in life.

> *"Before I formed you in the womb, I knew you, and before you were born, I set you apart . . . "*
> Jeremiah 1:5a (NIV)

Just as Jeremiah was known and set apart by God as a prophet, so is your child known and set apart for divine purpose. Even though my efforts with my students were as a teacher and school administrator, I was able to begin making inroads into their futures by using some of the same parenting strategies that had been tremendously successful with my own children. When God blesses parents with children, He gives "the best gift" and the "best gift" parents can give their children is a sense of purpose for their lives. The parent whose attitude, mindset and perspective is fixed on discovering their child's unique purpose is in a unique position to sow seeds of purpose in the hearts and minds of their children, and to dramatically impact the trajectory of their child's life. It is equally as true for guardians, foster, step, or adoptive parents, teachers, counselors, and mentors alike.

Are you now asking how does a parent go about discovering their child's purpose? I am glad you asked. The answer is simple, seek, ask, and knock. Seek God in prayer for insight, understanding, and revelation. Ask questions of your children. Discover their likes and interests. Knock on doors, identify opportunities, and activities that will aid in developing the skills, and temperaments your children will need to fulfill their purposes.

I have discovered that children will let you know exactly who they were purposed to become. Their purpose may not be as defined as the prophet Jeremiah's was, but again, it very well may be. I encourage parents to listen and observe your children with a discerning eye. Soon you will begin identifying and recognizing their strengths, natural gifts, talents, and abilities. Through conversation, observation, revelation, and interaction your child's purpose will grow increasingly more clear. Follow their lead and most importantly, ask. Ask God in prayer and ask your child what interests them. Understanding you have been chosen to help foster and develop the future destinies of your children will help you, as a parent, stay on task, remain focused and cut out a lot of the background noise that will present itself from time to time along your parenting journey.

Be careful not to impose your will over and against God's will for your child. Remember to not go overboard with the desires you have for your child which may not be the plan that God has. It is an area where parents make the mistake of pushing their will and desires on their children. Your most effective path forward is to balance both leading your child while following God's lead and their lead as well.

MINDSET MATTERS 5:
VISION IS THE ENGINE:

Purpose and vision can intertwine and frequently overlap conceptually. Knowing one's purpose and having a vision for one's life can be similar and easily used interchangeably in conversation. But, the two have separate and distinct meanings and functions. "Vision is the engine that propels purpose forward." One is not complete without the other. Vision is when you see "purpose" in your mind and then you begin to imagine. Parent, you are the visionary leader in your child's life, especially during their formative years. A visionary leader is tasked with the responsibility of ensuring the vision becomes reality. This is accomplished by stating clear goals, outlining a strategic plan for achieving those goals and equipping and empowering each child to take action on the plan. As visionary leaders, parents bring their child's purpose to the fore and then goes about the business of turning vision into reality. This is an incredible responsibility and you are the one who has been chosen to get the job done.

As you discover your child's purpose, develop a vision or long-term plan for your child's future. Provide the leadership necessary to move your child forward. Communicate the plan and purpose frequently. It is important for your child to have a sense of belonging, that their lives matter and have meaning so they are not condemned to an existence of wandering aimlessly through life in search of themselves. That they have an integral part to play in a bigger plan. Every interaction you have with your child must drip with the essence of this reality. Great potential is locked within each of your children. Create an environment where you are confident and supportive. Avoid the temptation of reliving your own life vicariously through them. This is your child's time. An environment where curiosity and creativity, exploration, individuality, and experiences encourage your child to begin filling in the finer details to their purpose as they get older. Parents, as visionary leaders, begin equipping, empowering, and encouraging their children early on—without delay. I cannot express how valuable taking this approach is and what a dynamic impact visionary leadership within the home has on the outcomes of children. It all begins, however, with parents having the proper mindset.

Proverbs 29:18 provides a explicit description of how life is when there is no vision. According to the original Hebrew text, the most accurate translation I was able to find is:

> *"Where there is no revelation, no*
> *prophetic insight,*
> *no vision,*
> *no seer or interpreter;*
> *the people cut loose, are*
> *stripped,*
> *made naked,*
> *lawless, perish,*
> *are unrestrained,*
> *cast off restraint and run wild."*

When a parent has no revelation from God or prophetic insight and lacks vision for their children, those children cut loose, are stripped of their potential, are made naked, are lawless. These children perish and are unrestrained, cast off restrain (rebellious), and run wild. Prophetic Parenting is the most intentional form of parenting in existence. There is no other parenting style that is more intentional and laser focused than prophetic parenting.

Congratulations on taking these first steps to become an even greater and more effective parent: stretching yourself, educating yourself, and reaching beyond your comfort zone to provide the best possible environment for your child to grow and thrive. I am excited for your journey! However uncertain, ill-prepared, or ill- equipped you may feel, keep in mind you are God's choice, your children are the best gifts, love without condition, allow God's purpose to guide you and your vision to drive you forward.

God will grant you the grace, wisdom, and capacity to become the highly effective parent you desire to be. Prior to becoming a parent, we each have experiences, fears, and baggage that we do not want carried over to the next generation. Half of the battle is won when we recognize the challenges, elevate our outlook, and fix our sights on being the one individual who will affect positive change in the lives of our children. Your story and experiences are likely quite different from mine, but I know that through renewing your mind, it will help you transform as a parent and become the parent you were created to be.

At the core of most parents' hearts is the desire to simply be a good parent. To love and to be loved by our children, and to know we have done everything within our power to cause them to be healthy, happy, well-adjusted, and successful. Through your parenting, your child will discover and understand the reason they were given life. It is the greatest gift a parent can give. What a joy it is to witness your child develop a sense of knowing that they are an integral part of a greater plan and purpose. One that is bigger than themselves. God is doing something incredible and extraordinary through you as a parent. Own it!

CHAPTER 6
PEELING BACK THE LAYERS

I was asked recently what made me an expert on parenting, that I would write a book and share my thoughts, systems, and experiences with the world. To this, I proudly responded, that the proof is in the eating of the pudding. In today's society, thousands of individuals present their untested, unproven philosophies on parenting. Some of whom have never had or raised children of their own—not of multiple children spanning over forty years. As I listen to their rationale and parenting advise, admittedly, some of their concepts have validity. However, in the grand scheme of things, their limited experience makes me pause, and I cringe understanding that the person or parent they are today will change dramatically over time. As well as the child they are parenting. There may be a few nuggets that can be gleaned from an inexperienced parent, however, it would not be wise to adopt an entire parenting methodology from one. My body of work spans over four decades beginning with observing, and training my Sunday school students, raising my own biological children, tutoring and mentoring children grades 1-12, counseling parents and families and owning my own K-12 home school co-op where I worked with parents and their children daily.

In 2004, I hosted the PROPHETIC PARENTING CONFERENCE, first of its kind. I invited Dr. Wanda Davis, a nationally acclaimed minister, teacher, prophet, life coach, and a best-selling author, who is now deceased; and Prophet Erik Cooper a pastor, speaker, and Spiritual leader, along with other teachers and trainers from across the country to speak on a variety of topics ranging from the importance of having vision for your children to empowering step, foster, and adoptive parents to raise children with passion and purpose. My goal was to introduce Prophetic Parenting to an array of parents and empower them to begin integrating this style of parenting within their households, and into their day-to-day interactions with their children.

At the time of the conference, my oldest two sons were thriving in college. One majoring in micro-biology, immunology, and biogenetics, and the other in film. They embodied all the hopes, dreams, and prayers I'd prayed for them over two decades prior. They were proof that prophetic parenting produces results! My youngest son was in high school at the time, carving out a path to college through his success in sports. Often narrowly, but avoiding, nonetheless, the gang culture that permeated his generation.

My youngest and only daughter was but six at the time, but by every indication, she would soon be on track as well. I desired so deeply to share this success and shout from the rooftops that a parenting method had been discovered had the potential to work extremely well in any given situation or set of circumstances. I felt I had hacked the code to becoming a highly effective parent, and my goal was to help as many parents as possible achieve the same or similar outcomes.

The purpose of the conference was to introduce parents to Prophetic Parenting as a highly effective parenting style. At the time, I was roughly twenty-two years into my parenting journey and had seen first-hand just how effective prophetic parenting methods and strategies had been with my children and other children under my care. We conducted workshops and breakout sessions. The auditorium was filled with parents from many different backgrounds and family histories. Some were birth parents and others foster parents, and even grandparents participated in anticipation of receiving some nugget of truth that would transform their effectiveness.

In this chapter I will draw comparisons between the parenting styles we explored earlier and the methodologies of Prophetic Parenting. You will be given an opportunity to see where and in what ways Prophetic Parenting aligns with and deviates from the top parenting styles. Although not an exhaustive list of the various styles of parenting recognized today by leading behavioral psychologists, the following descriptions will go a long way to provide a solid foundation and framework for each reader to begin carving out their unique form of prophetic parenting.

So, how does Prophetic Parenting compare with the parenting styles we explored previously? Is Prophetic Parenting a standalone parenting style or is it an "add-on" that compliments and enhances other styles of parenting? The beauty of Prophetic Parenting is that it is a robust and dynamic form of parenting that is solid enough to stand on its own merit while being practical enough as a spiritual turbo boost add-on to most any style of parenting. The only exception, of course, would be the Neglectful Parenting style for obvious reasons.

THE POWER OF PROPHETIC PARENTING

If being compared in methodology, practice, and application, Prophetic Parenting is most similar to the Authoritative parenting style with a healthy dose of the Authoritarian style of parenting. As you may recall, the Authoritative style of parenting has been defined as one that strikes a balance between being firm, warm, and supportive. Instead of focusing on children to mindlessly follow rules without explanation or collaboration, authoritative parents will discuss rules and expectations as a family. In like fashion, it is the environment that is also created within the Prophetic Parenting style.

As a family, prophetic parents are consistently clear on what the rules, standards, and guidelines for the family are, and go into detail explaining, describing, and giving relatable examples as to the reason the rules are in place. Within the prophetic parenting methodology, rules are designed for three primary purposes. One, the rules of the house are to protect the children from physical, mental, emotional, and even spiritual harm. Such rules draw a contrast between what is allowed to transpire in a prophetic parenting home in comparison to what may take place in a non-prophetic household, and is always coupled with mounds of explanations, examples, biblical accounts, and life lessons.

Rules within the prophetic parenting paradigm are rooted in and aligned with God's unique purpose for the child, the family, and the household. Several years ago, a world-renowned minister spoke of how her grandmother would, from time to time, call her indoors from playing with her siblings and friends to sit still for fifteen minutes. The minister shared how this perplexed her and how she questioned her grandmother as to why she had been called inside from playing while the other children had not. Her grandmother explained that one day, she would sit before kings and world leaders; and therefore, it was important for her to know how to sit still and conduct herself maturely.

Now, years later, the minister has traveled the world and has been in the company of heads of state, presidents, kings and world leaders.

Her grandmother "saw something" in the minister as a child and felt directed to nurture that purpose and cultivate her unique purpose with a set of rules that did not necessarily apply to any of the other children. It was striking that the grandmother did not require the siblings to participate in the same discipline. Had the minister become world renowned because of her being raised in a prophetic environment under a set of rules that were divinely inspired? I believe so. Parenting prophetically has less to do with the parent or, in this case, the grandparent being the ultimate, supreme authority in the child's life as much as it has to do with the will and purposes of God creating the environment and establishing the rules. Although this grandmother took her time to explain the reason for the rule, there was no compromise as to whether the rule would be followed or not. In prophetic parented households, aligning with God's word, His plans and purposes are not an option as they are directly tied to the future safety, protection, and success of the child. In this way, prophetic parenting may be viewed as leaning slightly toward the authoritarian style of parenting.

In lieu of an explanation, "Because I told you so," is listed as being a response authoritarian parents are likely to offer inquiring children who question or even demand explanation from their parents for the rules they have set in place. I literally laughed out loud upon first reading about the characteristics of authoritarian parents and finding this generation old response! If I had a dollar for every time my mother, aunt, or grandmother said, "Because I told you so," to me or one of my cousins, I would be a wealthy woman. In fact, for a child to stand flat-footed and challenge their parent's word or authority was viewed as being disrespectful to the ninth degree. It just was not acceptable and would not be tolerated. Needless to say, times have changed and children are far less concerned about being respectful or not stepping out of line with their parents as they were decades ago.

Although, within prophetic parenting there is absolutely room for children to question and seek deeper understanding and clarity regarding the regulation, boundaries, and rules the prophetic parent has put in place. There also exists a line the child is expected to respect and honor. In today's society, giving children the liberty to voice their opinions and demand explanations has gotten completely out of control in many instances. I have observed a child refuse to comply or obey their parents until an explanation acceptable to the child has been given and only until then, not before.

In Prophetic Parenting, woven within the parenting style is the mandate to teach, train, and explain, however, every so often, it is healthy to remind your little one of your role within the family as their parent-the ultimate authority. An occasional, "Because I told you so," helps to keep the scales balanced and reminds the child that as the parent, you do not owe them an explanation for each and every decision you make. Remember, authoritative parents and even gentle parents are still clear on who's in charge, and they do hold their children accountable when the child does not do what is expected. Authoritative parents and even gentle parents set limits and are responsive to the needs of their children. It is in alignment with the Prophetic Parenting style. Prophetic parents are warm, loving, responsive, engaged, and vigilant. Of the parenting styles, experts often consider the Authoritative style of parenting as the gold standard.

Now that Prophetic Parenting has been determined to be highly Authoritative with sprinkles of the Authoritarian Parenting style as needed, it is only befitting to compare prophetic parents to Professor Amy Chua's Chinese Tiger-Mother Parenting style. As I mentioned previously, Tiger Parenting is a style of parenting that instantly arrested my interest as it peels back an additional layer to reveal the heart, motives, and intentions of the parent themselves. From one mother to another, Professor Amy jumps right in and provides a glimpse into the tenacity and resolve of my sister, the Tiger Mother. The sheer determination and laser focus of the Tiger Mother resonate deeply with me and remind me of how fiercely focused and tenacious I was during my child rearing years. I had my set my eyes on the outcomes and allowed little room for deviation.

As soon as I read, "Tiger Parenting refers to a strict, authoritarian method of parenting that is meant to raise high-achieving children," I was captivated -- for this outcome is at the heart also of Prophetic Parenting as well although there are several significant differences in the approach. The goal of the prophetic parent is to raise motivated, purpose-driven, Christ-centered, high-achieving children as their success and accomplishments are their God ordained birthright and testifies of God's overwhelming ability to bring His promises to pass in their lives. Professor Amy goes on to describe that the Tiger Parenting methodology includes children foregoing sleepovers, parties and other leisurely activities to focus on their studies. Although the prophetic parenting methodology does not ascribe to quite a rigid set of standards, it does recognize the validity and effectiveness of certain activities being kept to a minimum.

When my children were young and throughout their teen years, partying, spending the night over their friend's houses were definitely kept to a minimum. This decision sits squarely on the parent's shoulders as to how liberal or conservative you will be with the social activities of your children. Again, rules and boundaries are designed to protect the child physically, mentally, emotionally, and spiritually. With the intent to preserve your child's innocence or focus, you may determine to monitor more closely or even eliminate certain activities and involvements until you are certain your child is mature enough to handle it. I understood that the culture desired to indoctrinate my children with worldviews and philosophies that were contrary to God's purpose for their lives. I also understood that I had a limited amount of time to embed those things that would be enduring, solid, and useful to them long term. I wanted to be the loudest and most influential voice ringing in their ears. As a result, I found ways to minimize outside influences.

Similarly, Tiger Mothers have a vision for their children. From Mindset Matters, we discovered that "Vision is the engine that propels purpose forward." Professor Amy Chua when discussing the over representation of Chinese students in many of the nation's elite universities, high SAT Math scores, and being disproportionately represented among U.S. National Merit Scholars, states that "it is all about parenting," and I absolutely agree. If a study were done of successful, high achieving individuals who were raised in an environment where the prophetic parenting methodologies were employed, I believe the numbers would be astronomical!

If there was a way to measure the number of men, women, and children from every walk of life and socio-economic status who trace their success back to a praying grandmother, a Sunday school teacher, pastor, God-parent, sermon or personal encounter with God, I believe it would be revealed just how potent the word of God has been in the lives of children, men, and women globally! Not just within my own family. To excel, achieve and succeed are the by-products of prophetic parenting and through this book, countless thousands and even millions of individuals will begin sharing their journey of how the Prophetic Parenting methodology dramatically changed the trajectory of their lives. The world needs to hear from each and every one and through this book a platform has been created for these testimonies to rise to prominence. While Professor Chua describes Tiger Parenting as purely power- assertive, studies show there is room for positive parenting strategies among many people who practice

Tiger Parenting. This is significant in that it demonstrates the power of positivity, care, and nurturing even when incorporated in the most stringent approaches to parenting. Based on Professor Chua's description of the Chinese Tiger parenting techniques she employed with her own children, however, I found Chua's particular authoritarian approach to parenting to be deeply disturbing. Chua recounts a particular incident when her seven-year- old daughter failed to master a new piece on the piano, Chua says she "drove her daughter relentlessly." "I threatened her and told her to stop being lazy, cowardly, self-indulgent, and pathetic." Amy, yelling and hurling one insult after another to her daughter, "no lunch, no dinner, no presents for Christmas, no birthday parties and on and on." Reading this account was mortifying! Her house became a war zone and that she made her daughter work into the night, denying her even a break to go to the bathroom," and that she had even 'lost her voice' yelling at her daughter. Amy believed her daughter would not learn the piece without intense effort, and that effort was not going to happen unless the child was pushed.

Prophetic Parenting sharply differs from this approach. Life within the boundaries of the Prophetic Parenting methodology is rich with discourse, discussions, discovery, explanations, teaching, and training. Using words or actions to degrade and malign children or tearing down their self-esteem is never acceptable. Prophetic Parenting is primarily word-based causing the parent to pay keen attention to the words they use even when scolding or admonishing their child. There is no room in prophetic parenting for making a child feel less than or using demeaning verbiage as though the child is not enough. Always keep at the forefront of your mind as a parent that your words carry incredible weight. Children hear the voices and the words spoken by their parents far into their adulthood. The words a parent chooses to use should be chosen wisely and not recklessly. Bitter and sweet water cannot flow from the same fountain. There is a delicate balance that parents must strike between pushing a child towards greatness and breaking a child's spirit. Yes, push your children to explore, expand and stretch themselves beyond their zones of comfort and complacency. Challenge your children to believe in themselves and not run away from opportunities that may seem at first to be beyond their abilities. The Prophetic Parenting style is careful to not cause harm or damage. However, the child's sense of self-worth is affected in the process. As frustrated as parents may become with their children along their journey, there are ways to address the child that builds and lifts their soul while also conveying that there is far more that they are capable of achieving and accomplishing. Make every effort to avoid lashing out in anger. You can never unring the bell or undo the damage done through words and actions motivated by frustration or anger.

Listen, I get it, this may be a tall order to fill at times. Make no mistake about it, emotions can and will run high and hot while parenting your child even under the best of circumstances. Inevitably your child is going to do or say or exhibit some behavior that is so unconscionable that, in the moment, you may lose your temper. Remember, I am not writing this book as an individual who has not raised my children. I have been there with each of my four children. To the best of my ability, however, when I felt myself wanting to lash out, I was purposeful in being careful not to say the damaging things that far too often are said and can never be unsaid. In those instances, when the circumstances push you to the brink, as the parent, you must possess the self-awareness to flip the narrative. Do not fall into the trap of speaking words that have the potential to crush or kill your child's spirit.

Countless times, I was on the verge of wielding the most hurting, destructive words my children could have ever heard from their mother, but instead, I used the moment to remind them of their strengths, abilities, and greatness. Oh, do not get me wrong, the moment was still intense and my voice elevated, but instead of hurling insults and personal attacks, I would make statements similar to, "As intelligent as you are, I know you can make better decisions than this!" Or, "God has so much more for you than what you are giving into right now! You've got to want it." "I know you haven't, so why are you behaving as though you have?"

As "on board" as I am with some of what Tiger Parenting represents and the rationale behind the parenting style along with the incredible outcomes, reading Amy's words to her daughter made me cringe. I was so shocked and taken aback and honestly could not believe what I was reading. Such verbal attacks can undercut and undo the work you are doing to build and support your child's efforts causing psychological fractures or weakness that, once they reach their teens or adulthood, could potentially lead to them loathing themselves or one day suffering from depression or experiencing feelings of worthlessness. I have heard and witnessed parents demean their children, calling them out of their names, using profanity, calling them stupid or ignorant, a fool, or telling the child they get on their nerves. "You never do anything right." Why are you so lazy?" "How is it you're always the one to mess everything up?" These are but a few examples of this negative, derogatory, dehumanizing speech. Parents, understand that your children are going to have enemies and experience isolation and rejection enough in the outside world, it is inevitable. As a parent, you never want to be counted in the number with the harshness of the outside world. Go hard to equip and train your child. Go hard to defend and advocate for your child, but never to damage or break their spirits.

Being stern without being destructive is an attainable goal. If you are a parent who has lashed out or said harmful things to your children or about your children you wish you could take back, this is your opportunity to chart a different course for yourself. Stop. Change direction and make yourself accountable to someone. You may even ask your child for forgiveness or let them know through your actions that you are a changed individual. Healing and restoration can begin at any age and at any time. Commit to it and be consistent, over time you will find your child will regain trust in you.

During my years working in education both as a teacher and as a family advocate, it was a proven fact that even within the classroom setting where high expectations are set and children receive positive encouragement to reach them, they rise to the occasion and excel. It's really that simple. Children will rise and fall often based on the standards and expectations of those around them. The philosophy of Prophetic Parenting is to setting the bar high, having boatloads of expectations for your child to attain, achieve, and even exceed expectations. Create a rich environment where your child is convinced they can succeed even with the most challenging tasks. It builds character, strength, fearlessness, and a strong sense of confidence.

Children raised under Prophetic Parenting methods are not only taught to become accustomed to working hard from an early age as is the case with Tiger Parenting, they are also taught to pursue attaining their God-given purpose as being the reason for their hard work. They are taught that there is a specific and unique destiny on their lives. They learn to be accountable, responsible, responsive, and respectful not only to their parents but also to individuals they encounter and interact with in the broader community and society at large.

With Prophetic Parenting, the parent is not the supreme authority in the household, the word and will of God is. Whether written or divinely revealed. These words may make some uncomfortable as we live in an age where individuals ascribe to all sorts of bizarre, harmful, unscrupulous impulses to being God inspired when actually they have not been. So, as prophetic parents are being led and directed by the Holy Spirit on how to raise, teach, mentor, train, and mold their children, they must also possess a firm grip on what thoughts and impulses are God breathed and which ones are not. For this very reason I have developed a Prophetic Parenting Mentorship Program that provides support, resources, and accountability for parents embarking on their own unique prophetic parenting journey.

Additionally, children raised under Prophetic Parenting methods are raised to understand there are diabolical forces at work that would hope to upend their progress and success. If there is a battle, the battle is not waged against the child but against the real foe. The one who seeks to destroy mind, soul, and body. It is a vitally significant aspect of prophetic parenting. Not only parents, but children must be acutely aware that there is an enemy whose primary objective is to kill, steal, and to destroy. This destruction is evident, plainly seen, and is manifest all around us. To equip and protect our children, prophetic parents warn and expose these tactics and devices of the enemy. To be forewarned is to be forearmed.

Children learning and developing an ear to hear God's voice is a part of the end game. Finding their voice and discovering their purpose is essential. It can only happen in an environment where views and thoughts, dreams, and visions of the child are discovered, identified, known and communicated. With Prophetic Parenting, although the parent is the one in authority within the household, the child and parent are both under the authority of God, His word and His way of doing things. This concept might seem a bit daunting, but it can actually be quite reassuring and stabilizing for the entire household. God has a plan for the lives of your children and He desires to inspire parents, equip, and empower parents to be the best version of themselves, and to provide the absolute best parenting tools and support along the way.

When my middle son was nineteen and my youngest seventeen, I found myself entering a space of constant stress and anxiety. I felt overwhelmed by my efforts to keep an eye on what they were involved in, where they were going and if they were safe. I did not want them to be taken advantage of or hurt, or led astray by the sly, crafty characters that lurk in the shadows awaiting the opportunity to seize and destroy them. Then one day, God spoke to my mind so clearly that I can still hear His words. He said, "Crissina, I know you love your children but as much as you love them (pause), . . . you will never

love them more than I do." I remember standing at the front door of the apartment just stuck in that one spot. Then the thoughts came to mind that God is omnipresent, everywhere at all times. He would be everywhere with my children no matter where they were night or day and that because of His love for them, God would protect them and keep them safe and keep them in remembrance of how they had been raised. I wanted their lives to be smooth and free of incidents that would be painful or hurtful. I was on the verge of becoming a hovering helicopter mom, and I was given peace that day.

It was ok to loosen my hold and to begin relinquishing my children into the hands of a more than capable God. Possibly due to my concern about their relationship with God remaining intact and the internal struggle I was experiencing letting go, the next words I heard were,

"Sometimes people have to hit rock bottom and see the enemy face to face before they ever lift their eyes to see and seek God." I did not want my children to hit rock bottom at any level; spiritually, emotionally, physically, or financially. My desire was for them to be spared the trauma and trials that are often encountered in life, but then I was reminded that it was in my lowest and darkest hour when God revealed Himself, His plan and His purpose in my own life. I could not stand in the way of the processes, circumstances and situations God would permit for my children to arrive at that same divinely inspired place where they would encounter God for themselves. It is the confidence, peace, and assurance parenting prophetically gave me and I am eternally grateful that God is faithful to His promises.

> *In this all-out match against sin, others have suffered far worse than you, to say nothing of what Jesus went through—all that bloodshed! So don't feel sorry for yourselves. Or have you forgotten how good parents treat children, and that God regards you as his children?*
>
> *My dear child, don't shrug off God's discipline, but don't be crushed by it either. It's the child he loves that he disciplines; the child he embraces, he also corrects.*
>
> *God is educating you; that's why you must never drop out. He's treating you as dear children. This trouble you're in isn't punishment; it's training, the normal experience of children. Only irresponsible parents leave children to fend for themselves. Would you prefer an irresponsible God? We respect our own parents for training and not spoiling*

us, so why not embrace God's training so we can truly live? While we were children, our parents did what seemed best to them. But God is doing what is best for us, training us to live God's holy best. At the time, discipline isn't much fun. It always feels like it's going against the grain. Later, of course, it pays off big-time, for it's the well- trained who find themselves mature in their relationship with God. Hebrews 4-11 (MSG)

Discipline is a normal, healthy, and necessary demonstration of love. Without it, a parent who cannot bring themselves to discipline their children is the parent who does not love their children enough to train them and prepare them for life outside their home. In other translations, Hebrews 13:5 uses the words chastens, scourges, disciplines, and punish to describe the ways God demonstrates His love for His children. Children desperately need to be exposed to the various aspects and manifestations of love, so they become well-balanced and well-adjusted psychologically and emotionally. When a parent only administers discipline but not nurture or only coddling without discipline child develops a warped view of what love is. Only equating or judging love through the lens of coddling or indulgences breeds weakness, and frailty causing the child to be ill-adjusted and unable to cope in the real world, misjudging sternness, or expectations as an indication the person does not love or like them. Parents, it bears repeating, a balanced measure between all the characteristics of love must be struck!

CHAPTER 7
FROM TOTS TO TEENS

In my forty-plus years of parenting, I have observed there is a direct correlation between how you parent your toddler and the teenager you will one day parent. In my experience, far too many parents ascribe to the misguided notion that once their children become teenagers, aliens take over their bodies, and the person the parent has known and loved for over a decade is non-recognizable. The teen who stands before you today is just the teen-sized version of the toddler who stood before you a decade earlier. Were you consistent with that toddler? Did you set boundaries with that toddler? Did you teach and train that toddler? Did you nurture, love, support, and affirm that toddler without condition? Did your toddler understand there would be consequences for their decisions? Were the consequences real or did you teach your toddler you were inconsistent, unreliable, and easily tossed to and fro and distracted? What did your toddler learn about your trustworthiness? Did you follow through on your promises?

Could your toddler count on you or on your word? Was your relationship with your toddler riddled with broken promises and idle threats?

Other than unconditional love, children need consistency. Consistency breeds a sense of security and stability. As much as they might protest, children crave boundaries and knowing there is someone in control who has command of the ship/household. I was graced to be raised by a community of women who understood this principle and through every conversation and demonstration they taught me to love my children lavishly, to be stern and unwavering when it counted most and to yield and be compassionate and caring when it was needed most. From watching and listening to the conversations of these women, most of whom were relatives or patrons of my mother's beauty salon, I learned that parenting would require a delicate balance of grace, tough love, and always being one step ahead of my future children. There was a common thread that ran through every household, parent by parent, and child by child. This thread represented the line. The invisible, indelible line these parents had drawn in the sand that no matter how young or old, their children understood that crossing it would rain severe consequences down upon their otherwise peaceful existence.

Through my research, I discovered a spot-on, comprehensive, easy-to-follow guide compiled by professional psychologists to help parents skillfully utilize authoritarian parenting to set a defined outer perimeter of boundaries within which all other parenting techniques, styles, and strategies flow freely. This team of psychologists, known collectively as Annabelle, is a mental health group practice providing therapy to adults, children, couples, and families. Their psychologists work closely with psychiatrists, pediatricians, and other professionals to provide holistic care to complex presentations. Setting boundaries early in life boils down to your child learning what acceptable behavior is and what is not according to Annabelle Psychology. Take a moment to review the list below that helps parents put the framework in place for setting boundaries.

1. Give Clear and Direct Rules
This leaves little ambiguity or loopholes. Your child is less likely to cross the line as it's easier for them to follow and understand the rules. Remember, they are still developing their language capabilities, too! Your language should be directive and close-ended, not open-ended or open for misinterpretation).

Tools/Techniques/Strategies: Children are wise beyond their years and will quickly seek out and identify weak links, inconsistencies, and loopholes to use to their advantage in playing one parent against the other or finding a way around the boundaries you are seeking to establish. Use definitive language when setting boundaries, not language that can be left up to interpretation or rules that are presented as though following them is optional.

2. Be Consistent. Consistency is Key
With consistency comes familiarity. By enforcing rules consistently, there is structure and discipline at home, both of which are important elements of effective parenting. It would be easier for your children to know how to stay within the limits that you impose on them. Moreover, they would also know that you are serious about the boundaries, which helps teach them about being accountable for their actions. Hopefully, this will make them think twice before they commit a (potential) transgression!

Tools/Techniques/Strategies: There are few things worse than for a child not to know which version of their parent they will be encountering at any given moment. Being lenient and lax one moment and then demanding and punitive the next can cause your child tremendous stress, uncertainty, and confusion. Think of boundaries as the non-negotiables within your relationship with your child. Your child should know precisely what the rules are and be met with the same firm stance each time they test or break a boundary. For your own mental health and the mental health of the child, be consistent. Consistency! Consistency! Consistency!

3. Appropriate, Congruent Body Language

We've all heard about how verbal language contributes only a small percentage of how convincing a message is. It applies to teaching children boundaries as well! When teaching or disciplining your child, give appropriate eye contact, speak with a firm voice, and have a neutral facial expression. Consider giving eye contact at their level, meaning that you have to stoop down not to intimidate them too much.

Tools/Techniques/Strategies: Body language is one of the most powerful tools a parent has when setting boundaries especially with toddlers. Toddlers need to see the change in your facial expression from pleasant and "business as usual" to a stern "I mean business" facial expression. More than raising your voice, the change in body language, and facial expression coupled with clear, decisive language often is all a parent needs to do.

Do not attempt to discipline them while still laughing or smiling at them—if you don't think that you would be convinced when someone does this to you, chances are, your child won't as well. As long as whatever you say is congruent with your actions, your child will understand that you're serious about what you say. It makes them more likely to keep within the set boundaries.

Tools/Techniques/Strategies: The goal is for your child to take you seriously and to know you mean business. While disciplining, training, teaching, or admonishing is not the time to play, tickle, laugh, do silly faces, or the like. In my experience and parental wisdom, to mixing the two only causes confusion in the child leaving them not being certain of and undermining the child's confidence in your authority as their parent. The time for your child to know when you are serious and to take you seriously begins at the toddler phase. Waiting until an older age will prove to be quite challenging. It is always best to begin correctly. Attempting to undo and reset is always terribly difficult.

One of the most effective disciplinary techniques I used when my children were quite young, was the "straight-face." Nothing arrests your child's attention more than the expression on their parent's face. Once my facial expression switched to a sober, serious, I mean business expression—I was then able to communicate knowing I was being heard and taken seriously. It is not "being mean," parents. This technique teaches your child that there is a time for fun and games and then there is a time for serious business. The two should never be confused. The lamest excuse for not disciplining their children I have heard parents say is, "I don't want them to be scared of me." Your child will not be scared of you unless you are being abusive. If you are a nurturing and loving, kind and playful, caring and attentive parent, setting boundaries and shifting your facial expression to a serious, no no-nonsense one, will certainly cause your child to develop a healthy respect for you and for whatever message it is you are conveying at the time. It communicates to the child that this topic is serious and important.

4. Remain Decisive and Follow Through with The Consequences

In an ideal world, our children will never be upset. Especially not with us. However, know that it's alright if your child is upset with you in the process of setting boundaries. They need to learn what is acceptable behavior and what is not. Moreover, the experience can also help them learn how to cope with negative emotions in a healthy, rational way. These lessons you have for them are very necessary, so don't feel bad for it. It can be tempting to withdraw whatever you've said or done but do know that empty threats are not the way to solve things, either. While they may make your child happy with you for now, empty threats just show your child that you are not serious about the boundaries. They might choose to defy these boundaries in the future.

Tools/Techniques/Strategies: One of the worse things a parent can do is give empty threats! Children are sharp and discerning and can discern relatively quickly when their parents are just blowing hot air. I have witnessed so many parents fall into this counterproductive behavior and it has not once turned out well. The parent loses control and battles to regain control after it is far, far too late. If a parent is not going to follow through with true consequences, it is far better to say nothing at all than to threaten and then not follow through. Doling out empty threats just teaches your child that you have no backbone and are not worthy of their respect.

5. Recognize When They Have Stuck by the Boundaries You Have Set

It is a great way to show your child that you still love them even though they did something wrong! When they're done something good, praise them, and acknowledge their efforts. Children love to be acknowledged and praised for something they did, especially when it's from their parents! This makes them feel loved and cherished. Thus, they will thus be more motivated to stick to these boundaries and feel these positive feelings again! Positive reinforcement is great at maintaining a child's good behavior.

Tools/Techniques/Strategies: I love this technique/strategy! It is actually a technique I used with my children that I knew had a deep, affirming impact. I called it, "I caught you doing right." Children migrate toward praise and recognition. They love knowing they are being seen that their good behavior has been recognized. This is another powerful, powerful tool in a parent's toolkit. Good behavior should be the norm, so praise or applause is not always required. But using this technique strategically and especially when your child least expects it can be highly effective!

6. Have Developmentally Appropriate Expectations

Understand what can be done at certain ages and what might be too advanced for your child. It prevents you from setting expectations that are too high and will save you lots of agony later. Look up what healthy expectations you can have for your child and use these as yardsticks for their growth. You can keep track of their progress and let them know about their improvement. It can also serve as motivation for them to continue sticking to your limits and exhibiting pro-social behavior.

Tools/Techniques/Strategies: Each child is different and their rate of development can be much different from that of other children at the same age. My encouragement is for parents to take the time to study their children. Make no assumptions and never, never, ever compare your child to any other child or to their siblings.. One of the core principles of Prophetic Parenting is to tailor your parenting around the unique bend and purpose of each child individually. Our goal is to build children from the inside out and to never tear them down.

7. Do Not Give Children Too Much Power and Control in the Family

Children develop an inflated sense of influence and authority when they are given too much power and control in the family. The boundaries that you've set for them get blurred. They might feel emboldened to test the limits set and will be less inclined to stick to what you've told them. This effectively sets the stage for future parent-child conflicts and power struggles when they grow older. Worse still, if not curbed from young, it might become more challenging to place limits on your child as they enter adolescence, which is a stage highly associated with independence-seeking and identity-formation. Loving our children means teaching them the right, albeit difficult, lessons to better navigate life, values, and relationships. Teaching them appropriate behavior happens to be one of these important lessons. We can start doing so in their childhood as they are keenly exploring their environment. Not only will an early head start help them in life, it will also make your parenting journey an easier one as time passes by.

Tools/Techniques/Strategies: Love your children enough to raise them the way they need to be raised. You are the parent and you are the one being held to account. Taking the easy way out never benefits anyone. Never fear losing your child because you are strong enough and secure enough to stand firm. Take it from someone who knows, your children will thank you later in life for providing them exactly what they needed, when they needed it whether they agreed or liked it or not. When you are strong, you are teaching your children how to be strong. Something I often told my children was, "If God wanted me to have friends, I would not have had to carry them for nine months." My point was that I had a job to do as a parent first and foremost; needing my child to be my friend could never be a consideration when maintaining boundaries. Friendship comes later.

Boundaries are not negotiable. Neither are boundaries up for discussion when being set or implemented. However, I strongly believe children should absolutely know and fully understand the reasons behind the rules. Inevitably, your toddler will challenge you and your authority as will your teen ager. Secretly, you child wants and needs you to stand your ground, be the enforcer, hold true to your conviction. The earlier this is established, the better. The morals, standards and perimeters set through boundaries are in place to keep your children safe, to protect them and mold the moral, spiritual and ethical aspects of your child's psyche. When challenged by one of your children regarding boundaries, you may in fact find yourself answering, "Because I said so" and there is absolutely nothing wrong with your child receiving that response from time to time. It helps them understand that their parent is ultimately the one driving the bus. You do not want to create an environment where every directive you give is questioned and won't be adhered to unless the parent 'answers' to the child.

I do not believe a parent can effectively train a child without answering questions and encouraging curiosity. Parents should want their child to feel they have a voice and can express their thoughts and feelings without retribution. But it is to your advantage and to the advantage in the long run for your child that every so often you remind them that they are you are the parent, and they are the child. If it is a matter of safety, ethics, consideration of others, and explain it to your child as often as necessary.

Enforcing boundaries provides parents with innumerable golden opportunities and teachable moments to shape and mold their child's behavior and character. It is best for the child and for the household if boundaries are established within the first few years of life. I learned this from my mother long before I became a parent myself. Over and over, my mother would say that parents have roughly six to seven years to instill boundaries, that after age seven, parents would be fighting an uphill battle. My modification incorporates my mother's philosophy and then expands the age to 12-14 depending on the child.

Toddlers are not the only ones who have tantrums. In my line of work and ministry, I have had countless opportunities to witness teens have tantrums as well. In fact, I have witnessed full grown adults fall out, yelling and screaming and giving themselves over to emotional outbursts as though they were still in the toddler stage of development. From my vantage point, such behavior is a clear indication that the parent failed to ring that person in and set consistent rules and expectations when the person was a toddler. Whether a teen or an adult, having tantrums or uncontrollable emotional outbursts are often an indication that this behavior was normalized during their younger years. Teen and/or adult tantrums and uncontrollable inconsolable outbursts carry with them an assortment of other dysfunctional and destructive behaviors that will likely plague their lives and the lives of any who become close to them.

If you have effectively parented your toddler by using the tools I have outlined above, the teen years will afford you the opportunity to gradually step back and help your teen to simply apply and reapply simply the training you have consistently provided since their toddler years. Raising a teen does not begin at age twelve or thirteen. It is a nugget of truth that you cannot afford to be lost on you. Effectively raising a teen effectively begins at age two. The parent of the toddler must parent with their teenager in mind. By being consistent, setting boundaries, loving without condition, understanding you are God's choice and have been handpicked as your child's parent while, having a vision for your child and raising your child to understand their purpose and begin to be driven by purpose will produce for you a well-adjusted, motivated, self-disciplined, low maintenance teen.

I lived this reality three times over as a single mother raising sons in the inner city. I could not wait until they were pubescent teens before I started molding and shaping them. There had to be a method to my madness from the jump. Consistently, this formula yielded my desired outcomes. Do yourself and your future household a favor. Rear your toddlers in such a way that by the time they enter their teen years, you will only need to support them, and on occasion, remind them of the tools you have instilled in them over the years. You're training the connective tissue that will anchor your teens soul, instincts, and core values. You will help your teen connect the dots—make the connections between what you have trained them through their pre-adolescent years and give them space for their personality to emerge.

Parents, through properly training and cultivating your toddler into pre-adolescence, you are unwittingly creating the environment to enjoy healthy, drama-free relationships with your teenager and young adult. I cannot emphasize it enough: with Prophetic Parenting, becoming a highly effective parent of a teenager begins when your child is two, not twelve.

In the following chapters, we go beyond the basics, delving into the intricate layers that compose the Prophetic Parenting style. Imagine a tapestry, woven with carefully chosen threads of belief systems and methodologies, forming the core of Prophetic Parenting. In these pages, I peel back the layers, offering you a glimpse into the inner workings of my parenting journey.

Transparent and honest, I reveal the driving forces behind every decision, and every technique. It's not just about sharing knowledge; it's about empowering you through candid conversations. Seeking clarity and deeper insights, you've arrived here. In **Nuggets and Nuances**, your quest finds fulfillment.

Here, you won't just gather information; you'll gain a profound understanding that resonates with your parental instincts. These pages echo with the whispers of essential truths, inviting you to explore the subtle art of Prophetic Parenting. Get ready; the journey ahead promises enlightenment, empowerment, and newfound confidence in your role as a parent. Welcome to the heart of Prophetic Parenting, where wisdom meets action, and transformation becomes tangible.

CHAPTER 8

A SNAPSHOT OF PARENTING WITHIN THE AFRICAN AMERICAN COMMUNITY

Before going any further, I would be cheating you of priceless perspective if I failed to share how my culture and community shaped me as a parent. As a woman of African descent, having been raised in and living in America, raising black sons and a black daughter in this country with its twisted, mangled past, there were certain unavoidable realities and dynamics that came to bear on me and on my children. Realities that have been passed from one African American household, to the next; from one enslaved or marginalized African to their descendants, and from one generation to the next. How our children conducted themselves, find the fortitude to rise above their circumstances, represent themselves in the outside world, carry themselves, and be articulate, educated, and cultured. The expectation and duty to do better than the previous generation. These are the considerations that have yoked the African American family together and the burden we all collectively bear.

These considerations bleed through in our parenting. It certainly did in mine. Hailing from under-served and marginalized communities historically, there is a knowing within African American parenting that we must raise our children to conduct themselves with more vigilance and self- awareness than their European and Asian counterparts. Knowing that their brilliance and genius often will be overlooked or even dismissed being defined by an expectation of being a problem, ineducable or plagued with behavioral and disciplinary problems. The African American parent spends countless hours reminding their sons and daughters that there is a necessity for them to jump higher, run faster, and reach further just to be seen, acknowledged, or even accepted by mainstream America. I was extremely intrigued by the research surrounding Tiger Parenting because, from my perspective, it closely resembles the parenting styles of families within the African American community as well. There is such a rich, cultural buffet of various styles of parenting that will influence the nuances of how you choose to parent your children. For me, that cultural influence hales from the African American Community.

When I searched for a comprehensive, detailed article on an African American parenting style based on African American culture, and the remarkably high occurrences of success and achievement that is produced as a result within our community; surprisingly, I did not find many. I found research on behavioral problems, poverty, delinquency, and the use of corporal punishment as it relates to parenting African American children, but I did not find much data that brought to the forefront the rich culture and approaches to parenting that have consistently produced the extraordinary outcomes that are prevalent within this community that are not dissimilar to those of the Chinese community.

Very little mention of the doctors, and lawyers, business professionals and financial powerhouses who were raised in single-parent homes by African American "Big Momma's" who cooked grits and fried chicken every meal and used the same chicken or bacon grease to knock the ash off of rusty knees and elbows. Little to no data on the African American artists and historians, musicians and educators who were raised at the knee of single black mothers working multiple jobs or side-hustles to keep food on the table and clothes on the backs of their children who were growing like weeds. I could not help but wonder where the studies were, where the research was that brought shine to the countless success stories that hale from the African American community at the hand of African American parents.

However, here's what I did find. According to Parenting In The Black Community, African American parents emphasize cleanliness, family ties, independence, obedience, religion, moral, and personal values, such as behaving well and respecting others, especially adults. According to In The Black Community: **Why Raising Children Is Different For Us** there is also a strong religious component to Black parenting when compared to white parenting. Another study conducted by the American Sociological Association reveals that regardless of social class, Black parents were more likely to send their children to Bible camp or Sunday school, while their white peers encouraged their children to participate in activities such as piano lessons and soccer camp. As an African American and a product of a cultural parenting style that many of my peers and I benefited from, I felt I strongly compelled to include and illuminate styles of parenting I believe are unique to the African American community. Understandably, I will not be able to account for every nuance of the African American experience and how parenting is influenced within this community, that is not the purpose of this book. However, I will share what I have observed, personally experienced and employed when parenting my own children.

When thinking of my childhood and my community, much of the parenting I observed and experienced was definitely centered on training just as with the Chinese community and the Authoritative Parenting style. I recall multiple conversations with my peers on the campus of my junior high school, where we would comment about a classmate not having "home training," which meant they were either rude, disruptive, disrespectful, or exhibiting behavior that our parents would not have tolerated and sternly corrected. "Home training" means exactly what you would imagine it to mean. It refers to the training, teaching, and discipline a child receives at home from their parents that prepares children to function in the outside world civilly and respectfully. My mother frequently said, "If you do not train your children at home in private, they will embarrass you in public."

An African American mother might be heard saying, "Behave yourself when you get over there." In my community, we all knew what those words meant because our parents had made it clear at home what behavior would and would not be tolerated. During my childhood and youth, I rarely saw African American children running wild inside restaurants, or movie theaters, churches, or other business establishments. It just did not happen, and the reason was, we had been trained at home not to do so, and we understood that if we did, there would be consequences. Consequences administered at home trains children to understand what the expectations of their parents are, when at home and especially when they are in public.

Home training is an incredibly powerful parenting tool that can be used at any time to remind and encourage your child that they are governed by a higher standard and expected to conduct themselves accordingly. Within African American culture, this process is often referred to as "the look." Frequently, when speaking to African American children or adults, in one form or another, their parents utilized "the look" to communicate without words when the child was getting ready to cross a boundary and enter the danger zone. Whether across church sanctuaries, in the principal's office, at a social event, or family gathering, African American parents possess within their "parenting tool kit" a certain "look" or facial expression that communicates to the child to make an immediate course correction, veering from their current actions, and realigning themselves with the expectations of their parent. The "look" is a wordless, voiceless warning that is only effective when clear expectations have been communicated and consequences have been laid out beforehand.

Because of the African American experience in the United States, African American parents historically share a common set of parenting values that instill strength, a grasp on realities beyond the control of the community, brilliance, strength, determination, discipline, self- reliance, and respect for oneself and for others. As a community, our history and experiences are rich and salient, and the way we parent our own children will inevitably find its way into any conversation, no matter the subject matter. Historically, one of the ways we [of African descent] love and bond with one another as a community is through storytelling and sharing our oral history.

VAN JONES INTERVIEW WITH BUSTA RHYMES

This was certainly on display when CNN commentator Van Jones sat down with rap star Busta Rhymes to discuss his newly released album.

I was well into writing this book and had already written my outline and notes for what I wanted to share about parenting within the African American community when I literally stumbled across the interview. I am not a rap enthusiast, and although I am from the generation that birthed rap music, before watching the interview, had I been asked, I would not have been able to name one Busta Rhymes song. I knew his name very well, but have lived disconnected from rap music and the rap scene for the most part. So, it is extraordinary that while in the middle of working on this book, I felt compelled to listen to this interview. Partially, the draw was due to my respect for Van Jones as a journalist and one who uplifts the African American community. So, I stepped away from my computer, and I watched. Roughly thirty-seven minutes into the interview, Van began asking Busta Rhymes about his relationship with his father and then asked how that relationship had impacted his relationship with his children. Van asks Busta Rhymes how he manages the toughness he experienced from his father as a child and his children.

Van Jones asks Busta Rhymes how he looks at his children considering how tough Busta Rhymes' dad was on him. Van wanted to understand if Busta Rhymes is more lenient than his father was or if Busta Rhymes employed 'tough love.' Rhymes unequivocally says that his approach to parenting was and is indeed tough. That he had followed in his father's footsteps in this way, especially when it involves respect and being well mannered. Being respectful of elders, adults, and especially parents is a huge component of African culture, not only here in the United States. African parents expect and even demand respect, even when the parenting approach is more open and our children are given the license to express themselves, voice their opinions or even disagree with their parents. I would venture to say that well over 90% of the time, the African American parent is going to require the child expresses themselves with a healthy measure of respect.

TRADITIONAL DO'S AND DON'TS WITHIN THE AFRICAN AMERICAN CULTURE:

1. It is not acceptable for children to argue or 'go back and forth' with their parents. Even if the family's approach to parenting is authoritative, that child understands that even where self-expression is permitted, there is an invisible line that is not to be crossed. I remember so clearly with my children, countless incidents when, while engaged in conversations and exchanges regarding a particular topic, I may have been engaged, listening intently, or even laughing and thoroughly enjoying the dialogue. Yet, as soon as something was said or was said in a way that crossed the 'respect' line, my facial expression would become void of expression, stoic, and firm, almost like a switch was flipped.

2. Nine times out of ten, within the African culture, you will not find parents permitting their children to call them out of their name, use profanity while speaking to their parents or refer to their parents in a profane manner. It is not going to happen! I remember hearing, for the first time, a classmate of mine speaking disrespectfully to his parents. We were in sixth grade, and I was attending a school that was nowhere close to being diverse. Over 95% of the 6th grade class was either Caucasian or Jewish with the remaining 5% being of African descent, Armenian or Thai. Culture shock would be the best way to describe my reaction not only as a result of

what my classmate said to his parents, and the tone in which he spoke to them, but also because of his parent's lack of reaction! I could not believe my ears or my eyes! Never, in my predominantly African American parochial school, neighborhood, or church had I ever heard a child speak to their parent with such lack of respect. "Who do you think you're talking to?!" In many, if not most African American homes, children have been asked this one, cure all question at least once during their childhood. With black families, it would be accurate to say, parents typically demand respect if nothing else.

3. The other behavior that stunned me when observing primarily European children with their parents, was hitting! I am not referring to the toddler who may hit playfully or even as an indication of displeasure. The toddler stage of development is when parents are afforded the opportunity to teach or train their children what is acceptable, and will be tolerated, versus what is unacceptable, and will never be tolerated. The hitting of parents certainly is a lesson that toddlers quickly learn is an unacceptable act that will never be tolerated. However, being in certain settings and witnessing children five years of age or older striking their parents, and then observing the parent assuming the posture of the overwhelmed, powerless victim caused the greatest shock of all! Hitting parents is unequivocally a level of disrespect that is in no way acceptable or tolerated

among the African American community. The atmosphere within the vast majority of healthy, African American households, will never permit for a child to raise their hand, and hit their parent.

4. Lastly, when Busta Rhymes listed 'manners' as also being a nonnegotiable within his household with his children. It rung so true as indeed being the second most important parenting priority within the African experience here in the United States, and elsewhere. I could literally hear my soul reverberating with the voices of countless generations, mothers, fathers, grandparents, and great-grands firmly requiring children being mannerable, respectful, honoring their parents and conducting themselves soberly, wisely, and with integrity are all rooted in biblical principles. Recently, I have had a number of conversations with younger parents within my community regarding the freedom afforded the popular culture, and the freedoms their children are afforded by not being constrained by traditional African or African American restrains as it relates to behavior or manners. There appears to be a school of thought developing where a few Gen-Xers but quite a few Millennials are considering and contemplating being far less vigilant or less intentional with their children than their parents were with them with respect to having a high expectation for good manners. With Prophetic Parenting, at its core, ascribes to biblical tenets, teaching, and training children to be both

respectful and mannerable is a significantly high priority behind the unconditional love, purpose, and the vision of the parent. Good old-fashioned home training will never go out of style.

As Van and Busta conversed, another topic heavily influenced by African American culture emerged. Van began describing a conversation he'd had with his children's mother, who is not of African descent, and the pushback and blowback he was experiencing surrounding his stance on training their children with the same cultural influences from the southern, African heritage he had been raised with. Then, Busta shared he had the opposite experience being that his children had the benefit of being raised, in part, by Busta Rhymes' mother who maintained cultural consistency, and even reinforced the values that Busta felt important to be passed on to his children. This is another conversation that is far more prevalent now than it had been in times past. Families are comprised of parents and grandparents who hail from diverse backgrounds and experiences. As a parent, it would serve you well to consider the cultural aspects of your parenting style, and the various cultural dynamics that will certainly impact your parenting style. Prophetic Parenting is the only style of parenting that transcends culture. When parents agree to follow the prophetic parenting model, there exists a greater opportunity for a unified approach.

Here are two celebrated African American men, from two completely different life experiences on one hand but unified culturally at their core, and in their philosophy and approach to parenting. I am incredibly blessed to have discovered their brief, yet powerful, three-minute discussion hidden within their one hour and forty-seven-minute-long conversation. How truly powerful of a moment it was to have two African American men, one from the academic world, and the other from the rap world, sitting together discussing and agreeing on a style of parenting that is the earmark of the African American community.

This conversation was golden and thoroughly described what I and multiple thousands of my peers and community members have recounted over the decades about their childhoods as well, being raised by African American parents. At some point in their conversation, Van recounts him saying these words to his children's mother, "Look, there are about seven to eight words that separate a civilized person from a heathen: 'Yes sir,' 'No ma'am,' 'Thank you,' 'Please,' 'You're welcome,' etc. "We're going to fight til the last dog barks on that." Van went on to give his reasons for taking such a hard stance on this particular aspect of parenting which is deeply rooted in African culture.

Raising respectful, well-behaved children is deeply imbedded in our DNA for a number of different, and converging reasons. It was so interesting that Van used the word heathen. I am not certain any other group of people make the reference to their children not conducting themselves as heathens to the degree that African American parents do. I distinctly recall my mother and grandmother using the same word, ". . . do not go out there [in the world] behaving like a heathen as though I have not taught you how to behave yourself." Children behaving as though they are untrained, godless or uncivilized was, and still is a huge component of parenting within the African American community.

As I mentioned earlier, I have no interest in rap music and although I am familiar with Busta-Rhymes' name, there was no logical reason for me to stop what I was doing, and invest my time into listening to the interview. My best guess is that my spirit drew me. It was important for me to hear these two Black men, discuss their approach to parenting. Better than I could articulate it, their conversation encapsulates the parenting experience with the Black community. This interview provides the perfect backdrop for me to share an encounter I had with my daughter when she was roughly four years old.

"You are a Christian, NOT a heathen!" were the words that rang out across the church social hall after the worship service one sunny, Sunday afternoon. Sunday service had just concluded and as the congregants began to disburse, many found their way to the church's social hall located at the rear of the sanctuary. After enjoying a powerful, uplifting worship experience and sermon, a soft, gentle buzz of joyous chatter filled the room as parishioners greeted one another and began fellowshipping.

Suddenly, there was a loud burst of activity with elevated yells and squeals as a band of children tore through the social hall. Laughing, yelling, charging at full speed completely free-wheeling, and uninhibited as though they were out on the playground. The sudden and abrupt activity captured the attention of us all, so, like every other adult in the room, I looked only to see my four-year-old daughter leading the pack, running at full speed in and out of the back door, and through the social hall again.

From somewhere deep within my soul, rooted in my family history, came those words that hung in the air like ripe, low-hanging fruit. For a brief moment, there was complete silence followed by a return to the moderate hum of fellowship. All the children stopped dead in their tracks briefly, and my daughter walked over to me, looking both stunned and bewildered, awaiting me to give her an explanation and instruction. Running and playing, squealing and yelling were fine and fit for outdoor play, but indoors, my standard demanded there be a certain decorum and a level of consideration for others which required an adjustment in behavior. This is what I shared with her as she and her playmates took their activities outside.

My daughter and I laughed about this just the other day. Twenty years later she says she can still hear my voice speaking those words that day. Had I planned to use those particular words? No, not at all. I do not recall ever using them with my older children, at least not drawing the contrast between heathens and Christians. Admittedly, I was a bit shocked when the words came soaring from my lips. They were spoken with such conviction, authority and power, I believe at that moment all my ancestors were speaking through me to my daughter as well. I seized that critical moment in her early development to lay the foundation that she would stand on for the rest of her life. Of course, she stopped running through the social hall, and took her activities outside where her typical childhood behavior was acceptable and appropriate. On the ride home that Sunday afternoon, I shared with her what the distinctions were between being respectful, and disrespectful, being disciplined and undisciplined, honoring God's house and honoring others and being wild and out of control.

In exploring the dynamics of African American parenting, it becomes evident that an overwhelming number of successful, accomplished African American individuals will attest to having roots in households where the foundational tenets of Prophetic Parenting were embraced. Whether reared by birth parents, grandparents, aunts or uncles, these influential figures were deeply shaped by the transformative impact of Prophetic Parenting principles. Our African American heritage is inherently spiritual, marked by unwavering faith, tenacity, resilience, and discipline. These virtues have not only enabled us to endure immense challenges but have also empowered us to thrive against seemingly insurmountable odds.

THE POWER OF PROPHETIC PARENTING

When considering influential and highly successful figures within the African American community, often you will hear them describe the influence of their single mom or praying grandparents who loved them, prayed for them, raised and trained them to become the person they currently are. Prophetic Parenting within the African American community is especially prevalent. It becomes clear that a deeper examination of this approach within the African American community is crucial. Exploring this method by behavioral psychologists and other researchers through academic research holds the promise of unveiling the profound wisdom inherent in prophetic parenting. Such exploration can serve as a wellspring of inspiration and guidance for countless families in our community. By delving into these principles, we have the opportunity to kindle a beacon of hope, nurturing a legacy defined by strength, resilience, and triumph for generations to come.

CHAPTER 9

TRAINING WILLS

In the words of behavioral psychologists, the way parents attempt to control and socialize their children transpires as a result of the parenting styles they choose to employ. Parenting styles, in their words, have a "significant impact on children's psychology." Outside exposures, experiences, traumas, and outlets will doubtless also have some influence as well, but by large, it is the style of parenting a child experiences within the home by their parents that will have the deepest, most long-lasting effects on a child's psychology.

Psychology is the scientific study of the human 'mind' and its functions, especially those affecting behavior in a given context. Psychology is also defined as the mental characteristics or attitudes of a person, group; or mindset. Psychology is further defined as the science of mind and behavior, which is the mental and behavioral characteristics of an individual or group. Prophetic parents are keenly aware of the role they play in training and shaping their child's psychology; to train and shape their child's mind, their wills, emotions and motivations. To control their behavior. Yes, parents! Controlling your child's behavior is a significant component of your role as a parent. No one enjoys being controlled, least of all your child. However, what you must understand and be able to distinguish between are the healthy, liberating aspects of control versus the abusive, stifling aspects of control. Parents must discover ways to operate in healthy, productive forms of controlling their child's behavior and shaping the mind. It is achieved through positive affirmations, healthy conversations, and setting fixed boundaries while comparing and contrasting the various causes and effects of their behavior. Children need an explanation in order to gain an understanding of how their actions, behaviors and decisions affect themselves and others. The way parents parent their children has a direct and indelible impact on that child's mental, emotional, and behavioral state of being in the present and for the rest of their lives. Understandably, this realization can be daunting and overwhelming for any parent. Do not shy away from the weight and gravity of your responsibility as a parent in this area! In fact, run toward it. Embrace it and know that with God's help, you are capable of being highly effective.

Knowing which techniques, approaches, and strategies are available to parents aid them in training their children without breaking their child's spirit or retarding their individuality and creativity? The goal here is not to break children down until your child is a timid, mindless, subservient creature who bows and cowers in your presence. It is not at all the goal. The desired outcome is for your child to become self-aware and understand how their decisions, actions, and behaviors work for their benefit and for the benefit of others or for their demise and for the harm of others. Training wills

Training Wills

are not an "outside-in" or "top-down" approach, but rather, goes directly to the heart of children and approaches training them from the "inside-out."

Humans are tripartite beings and free moral agents. We are spirits, we have a soul, and we live in a body. We have been granted the freedom to choose between right and wrong. Some have said that humans are spiritual beings having a human experience, and I largely agree. After all, God is spirit, and we were made in His image and in His likeness. But, as humans, we also possess a soul. Our soul is also comprised of three parts consisting of our mind, our will, and our emotions. The seat of our emotions, which is within our soul, is commonly referred to as our heart. Understanding this will go a long way in helping you train your child in a healthy manner.

Often, in this human experience, our emotions can carry us to the extreme in one given direction and our mind to the opposite extreme. It is our will that provides balance or an equilibrium between our mind and our emotions so we are balanced and consistent and not swinging back and forth from one mental or emotional extreme to the other. I like to describe the soul as being made up of the mind that is bent toward cognitive functions such as thinking thoughts, imagination and analyzing with emotions that are bent more toward our heart, our feelings, and our desires, and then our will or our "decision-making center" resides between the two judging, weighing, making determinations and decisions often based on our conscience. Our emotions and mind or thoughts chatter on and on, but our will is what stabilizes us. Knowing who we are, why we are and what we will and will not do is what makes us who we are and is what shapes how we present ourselves in the world.

Because our style of parenting has such a significant, scientific, and spiritual impact on our children's short-term and long-term mental, Emotional, and behavioral health, it would behoove parents to take the time to understand just how material your role, actions, and reactions are. Recently, one of my grandsons began screaming and crying at the top of his lungs. He had been playing with his brother, and within a split second his laughter turned into wailing. I asked him what happened, and he could not answer because his emotions were completely overtaking him. I calmly explained to him that I could neither help him nor resolve the issue if I did not know what happened. I needed him to calm down, find his voice, and articulate what had upset him. It took him a moment, but slowly, he could collect himself and communicate exactly what had upset him. I was able to address the matter and order was restored. From this exchange, my grandson discovered a more effective way of handling stressful situations, and he and his brother went back to playing.

I made sure he knew that I genuinely wanted to help and that I had the ability to help. I only needed him to reel his emotions in enough to verbalize the reason for his distress. In so doing, he learned that communication is the most effective route to receiving the intervention or relief he desired. Screaming at the top of his lungs was not the most effective route. His brother had taken a toy he had been playing with, and his feelings were hurt. He then became angry which caused these emotions to erupt. The goal is not for our children to be void of emotion, which is also an unhealthy state of being, but rather, the objective was for my grandson to hear and to know that he had options beyond screaming that would give him the results he desired. He needed to be heard, and I needed to demonstrate to him that I was interested in hearing and understanding what he was feeling at the time and why. My goal was to create an environment where he understood his voice, and his emotions were heard and understood; he would then be empowered to communicate with far less emotion and his problem could be solved. This brief exercise spoke to my grandson's will; his decision-making center, empowering him to manage his emotions enough to make the decision to stop crying long enough for the matter to be resolved. This type of training of wills (decision-making centers) begins, and is most important during the toddler stage. If parents are consistent, over time, the child will learn that emotional outbursts do not yield the best results, and exercising a little self-control can go a long way. Training wills begins young and early. Training in this critical area literally takes place each and every day over the course of your child's childhood. While under your care, you will have innumerable opportunities to mold, shape and refine your child's will that includes using many different strategies and tactics over countless various scenarios and sets of circumstances.

One of my more profound examples is of a role playing exercise I was inspired to have my oldest son take part in when he was around nine years old. We were walking home from his school, and I felt directed to create a role play activity with the objective being him focusing his attention on arriving at the front door of our home no matter what obstacles attempted to distract him or derail him along the way. I played the role of the distractions. As he walked, making progress towards the house, I would nudge him, slowly but firmly applying pressure to push or pull him from his path. I would speak the names out loud of the various possible distractions that he would encounter along his journey in life that had effectively derailed so many others from achieving their goals and reaching their potential, such as drugs, alcohol, gangs, seduction, partying, etc. "Hey, try these drugs; let's get high." "Aww, come on. Let's party." "Hey you, you're cute. Come on, let's go in the opposite direction together."

My goal was for him to hear and become aware of the myriad of different tactics the enemy would use to get him off track in life. In this moment, and by stringing together hundreds of other similar "light-bulb moments," I was equipping him with the tools he needed to set his sights on his goals and fortify himself against distractions that would inevitably arise. Most importantly, this exercise served to equip him to be the master of his own will and to not allow any external forces to dissuade him. Anyone who knows my children can attest to the fact that they are not followers. They stand firmly in their convictions and are rarely influenced by outside pressures. This was not an exercise I'd read about or heard about somewhere, in the moment it simply occurred to me to do. Now, thirty years later, my oldest son still remembers that day and has lived his life with that exercise in mind. These are the far reaching and long-lasting effects of Prophetic Parenting and the power of parents taking care to mold the minds, train the wills and sculpt the long-range behaviors of our children.

Prophetic Parenting focuses on shaping the conscience of children, equipping them to make judgment calls and decisions that are honorable, right, respectful, and considerate of others. Have you ever met someone that you would describe as not having a conscience? What caused you to view them in this way? Were they cold, uncaring, and without compassion for others? It is our conscience that considers right from wrong and guides us when it comes to making the right (righteous) choices in life. Our conscience helps us choose behaviors based on our morals and to develop a code of ethics that will govern our lives. It is through the conscience that God's voice is heard. It is through the conscience that God speaks to us and influences our behaviors and decisions. Have you ever made a decision that violated your own conscience and later experienced guilt, shame, or regret? Most of us have. The conscience pushes people to do the right or righteous thing. What is your conscience telling you? Years ago, I heard one of my instructors say that it is a parent's responsibility to "shape" the conscience of their children. Prophetic parents are in the business of training wills and shaping their children's conscience to recognize God's voice and to follow His voice once it is heard. It is our duty.

Indeed, parents are accountable to God and are charged with a tremendous responsibility. Earlier, we took a brief look at Chaio Shun, the authoritarian variant of "Tiger Mothers.' "Chaio Shun emphasizes harmonious family relationships—not the domination of the child and emphasizes teaching and training children in the appropriate or expected behaviors or morals." When I first read these words, I literally shouted, "Yes!!" This aspect of parenting had also been an enormous aspect of parenting within my community as well! I cannot begin to tell you how many times I would hear a mother or father of African descent emphatically reminding their child that they were NOT the boss of the home or ruler of the household! "Who do you think you are talking to? I am not one of your friends. You better change your tone. You are not running anything here, sir/ma'am!"

Then I began thinking of all the instances when I'd witnessed parents being kicked, hit, screamed at, manipulated, dominated, and controlled by their toddler or teenager. I recall thinking how "out of control" and "upside down" these parents had allowed themselves to become. Prophetic Parenting folds in the moral and spiritual components of the parent's responsibility to train in addition to the behavioral components as well. The onus of responsibility is clear. It rests squarely on the shoulders of parents to train their children and train them to abide by a code of ethics, behavioral standards, and morality. What distinguishes individuals from being rude and ruthless, brutal and abusive, and introduces morality to our existence is God or a God-consciousness. Humans, by nature, are neither good nor righteous. We are all born with a bend toward self-satisfaction, self-indulgence, and self-preservation above all else. When was the last time you witnessed a parent having to teach their child to be selfish, self-serving, to lie, push another child, hit, or spit? These proclivities are aspects of the fallen, sinful human condition, and exist within us all. In psychology, Freud describes this aspect of the mind as the "ID," which he describes as the primitive, self-serving, and instinctual part of the human mind. I am presenting to you that your child's "ID," their mind, will, and emotions can be trained through instruction, demonstration, and practice over time.

In Proverbs 22:5,6 we find recorded,

> *"Thorns and snares are in the way of the obstinate [for their lack of honor and their wrong-doing traps them]; He who guards himself [with godly wisdom] will be far from them and avoid the consequences they suffer. Train up a child in the way he should go [teaching him to seek God's wisdom and will for his abilities and talents], Even when he is old, he will not depart from it."* (AMP)

As a kid growing up in church, each time I heard or read this verse, my attention would immediately be drawn to the phrase "in the way he should go." I did not get the sense that the fullness of the verse was widely understood or that most adults knew exactly how to achieve its full admonition. As parents, how do we train our children in the way they have been purposed to go if we do not somehow seek to know and discover their God-preordained way? At the forefront of Prophetic Parenting, is the necessity that parents first have insight into the path God [their creator] has intended their child to take.

Then, create a "roadmap" of sorts or style to train their children up in the bend of their God-given purpose. In Job 23:10 Job says,

"But he knows the way I take." (NIV)

God knows the way, God knows the path, God knows the direction, God knows the purpose, God has given the talents, God has given the aptitude, and the abilities that compliment and accompany your child's purpose and mission in life. So, it only makes sense for a parent to seek, consult, and converse with God for the tools, techniques, strategies, and systems that would be best suited for that particular child. The requirement would be for a parent to actually have specific conversations with God about His plan for their child's life, and then be led and directed by God to effectively train their child in "the way they should go." Many of us do not have conversations with God regarding God's purposed path for our lives, yet alone the lives of our children, so it is understandable that so many parents feel at a loss, overwhelmed, frustrated, and confused.

A newly coined alternate approach younger parents now ascribe to is to choosing to do nothing. To simply not take responsibility to train their children, and to rather opt-out leaving their children to "figure out their path on their own," when God's word clearly requires the parent to train the child in the way they should go. Standing idly by and permitting children to figure out their path, purpose, and life on their own, may sound trendy and cool but in actuality, the parent who takes this position is being negligent, and derelict in their duty of providing their children with guidance, instruction, and direction. It is unconscionable, and is in diabolical contradiction to what God has commissioned us to do, and be as parents. It is our God-ordained responsibility to teach, mold, guide, direct, and shape the tender hearts, and minds of our little ones toward God, and toward the purpose God has intended for them. You can do it! God would not require you to accomplish an assignment you are not capable of accomplishing. God is not cruel or unjust and He does not set us up for failure. Remember, you are God's choice for this job and He will gift, grace, and equip you to rise to the occasion.

Once, I began wrapping my mind around the magnitude of my responsibility. I recall saying out loud, "I do not know which way they are to go. Only You [God] do!" "[God] You have to show me their 'way.' Show me what You had in mind when You created them and gave them life." It is the posture each successful, highly effective parent begins their parenting journey. A posture of humility and a willingness and openness to learn and grow through the process. I wanted to know and understand that through seeking knowledge and wisdom through prayer and the word, the information was available and accessible. To access it, I simply needed to ask. Little by little, as the days, months, and years passed, I would receive little glimpses and glimmers of what I believed God had in mind when He created my children, and gave them to me to raise. If there were details and specifics concerning my children available, I was determined to access them so I could use that information to inform my approach to parenting that particular child.

As a result of my vulnerability and willingness to listen and learn, God honored my prayers, and began flooding my heart and mind with inspiration, information, and insight regarding the long- term destinies He had predestined for my children, and He will do the same for you as well.

As aforementioned in the chapter, 'Mindset Matters,' the core of Prophetic Parenting is to give the child a sense of their unique purpose long before they reach adulthood. Raised in my mother's beauty salon where, as a child, I was privy to the conversations between middle-aged women who described their marriages, their jobs, their finances, and too often, their frustrations and disappointments with their adult children. I remember the hurt and utter disappointment that welled up in their hearts and flowed through each word they uttered.

I remember feeling sad for them as they described their child's lack of motivation and direction or their decisions to live lives that brought grief and pain to their parents. Trying to find themselves. Wandering aimlessly through life, bouncing from one thing to the next, dabbling in one thing or the other in search of their identity, in search of where they fit in the grand scheme of things and for the meaning of life. Parenting prophetically provides your children with a sense of who they were created and predestined to become well before they reach adulthood. Certainly, there will always be some specifics and details that will shape their lives that may not be in full view initially as they come into their own, but there is a distinct difference between the process of "coming into your own" as a mature adult, and one who is lost, and "trying to find themselves."

Training the wills of your children shapes their conscience, their temperaments, their decision-making processes, their moral compasses, and prepares them to fulfill their God-ordained purposes. The two are tied to one another. This responsibility rests squarely on the shoulders of parents. Yes!

CHAPTER 10
THEY'RE JUST KIDS!

Only here in the United States have I seen such a concerted, intentional effort to amuse and entertain our children to death. Literally to death. Somehow, in this Europeanized Western culture, parents are bombarded with the erroneous philosophy and belief system that children are mindless, incapable beings who lack the capacity or capability to function in an environment where they are not being coddled, doted upon or removed from the challenges and struggles of day-to-day life. Here's what I am not saying. I am not saying that parents should not protect their children from situations and circumstances that are harmful, dangerous, and abusive. Absolutely, it is the role and responsibility of parents to create a buffer between the damaging, destructive occurrences in life and their children. To take on responsibilities and become the answer to the problems that are simply a part of the real world in which they will one day live. In every other culture that I have studied and witnessed, children are given responsibilities within the family structure. They are taught and trained to be a viable, functioning, contributing member of the family for the growth, stability, and success of the family at large.

If you recall in the chapter, 'Parenting With Style,' the attributes of an Authoritarian Parenting style and a Tiger Mother parenting style were listed to include high standards, high expectations and an elevated expectation for maturity. The same is true for the Prophetic Parenting style as prophetic parents turn to the word of God to glean and understand parenting from a biblical perspective. Prophetic parents embrace the patterns, precepts, and processes that are laid out in scripture and apply them to their day-to-day actions and interactions with their children.

In Jeremiah 1:5-8, God speaks to a young Jeremiah age ranging between 13 and 17 years of age and says,

> *"I knew you before I formed you in your mother's womb. Before you were born I set you apart and appointed you as my prophet to the nations." "O Sovereign Lord," I said, "I can't speak for you! I'm too young!" The Lord replied, "Don't say, 'I'm too young,' for you must go wherever I send you and say whatever I tell you. And don't be afraid of the people, for I will be with you and will protect you. I, the Lord, have spoken!"* (NIV)

Raising children in a "fairy-tale" environment, unbeknownst to most parents is one of the most damaging, counterproductive, and destabilizing environments a child can be raised in. Only in the United States do parents feed an endless flow of amusement, toys, gadgets, videos, and games that are designed to capture and captivate young minds creating a skewed and distorted view on life. Children whose parents succumb to the marketing frenzy of big business and buy into the belief that a world overly saturated with amusement and fantastical fairy-tales is the reality children need to be happy and well- adjusted could not be further from the truth. Creating alternate realities for young, impressionable minds gradually undermines your child's ability to cope with real life or function in the real world.

Parents, especially parents raising children in the United States must realize they are in a capitalistic society that is driven by greed and boosting the bottom line. What is in the best interest of your child's overall mental, emotional, and spiritual health is not their concern nor is it their priority. Creating the illusion of the brain numbing and spirit crushing euphoria your child will experience if you purchase their products, is. Only in the U.S. will you find children who are fed in excess, clothed in all the latest styles, residing in more than adequate housing, with access to the latest and most innovative toys, games, and computer gadgets state that they are board. That they feel empty, unfulfilled, and struggle with wanting to live or take their own lives.

To my statements, many parents would rebut, "They're just kids!" I have heard these words a few times during my parenting years when other parents made their case for the reasons they felt compelled to take a looser, laissez-faire approach to parenting in comparison to the Prophetic Parenting approach I ascribed to. Where has loose and laisses-faire gotten us? Where has all the fairy-tales and fantasies gotten us? Where have all the tutus and unicorns and rainbows gotten us? Where have all the false and alternate realities gotten us? When our children emerge from the intoxication of the "make believe world" their parents created supposing to guard their children from the realities of life, where do they go? How do they adjust? Where do they run to recapture the fantasy? Plain and simple, parents. Your children need to know there is conflict in the world, that life is not always going to bend to their wants, whims, and wishes.

Children desperately need to feel the discomfort of conflict and learn the tools of resolving that conflict without feeling as if "their world is falling apart." I must say this, we live in a world now where little children are suffering from anxiety, depression, are suicidal, and homicidal. They are unable to cope or mentally process being denied or told "no." We have produced a generation of children who are so codependent on the opinions of others that they will cut themselves and even kill themselves or others because of being rejected, criticized, or ostracized. What are we doing as parents?! How have we allowed ourselves to become so far removed from the things that matter most? In saying children "are just kids," we are underestimating their awareness and capability to begin operating in their God-given purposes at incredibly young ages. It is where parenting prophetically differs from the "they're just kids" philosophy. It flatly does not line up with what has been spoken or demonstrated in scripture.

My children, like countless others went to amusement parks and played video games; skateboarded, went bicycle riding, to the arcade, to the movies, Chuck E. Cheese, and engaged in a number of other activities tailored for children. So, there is no need to brace yourselves expecting me to drop some extreme, radical bomb or take a hardline position on all entertainment and amusement. Not at all. The point and perspective I desire you to understand is that your children are NOT just kids—they are so much more! Your children are people or "very young, young adults."

They're Just Kids!

I was quite young when the call of God on my life began becoming clear and when God started using me in ministry. Consequently, I believe children can begin moving into purpose at very young ages. I also believe God desires to develop relationships with children at the earliest possible ages and has settled on His purpose for their lives even before they are born.

What I want you to know is that I have been blessed with the privilege of impacting young lives for the last 45 years. Beginning in 1976 as a Sunday school teacher, to raising my children through the 1980s and 90s, serving as a youth pastor for a number of years, working as a kindergarten, and first grade teacher to owning my own K-12 school. My entire life I have loved children and early on developed the philosophy that children are more capable and more adept spiritually than many adults give them credit for. As an educator, as a mother, and as a minister, my approach to my children, and to hundreds of other children over the years, has been to approach children as outstanding, bright, brilliant, capable, and anointed spiritual beings. Remembering that children are God's perfect gift.

Parents, do not underestimate your child's ability or God's desire to use them at young ages. During my years of parenting, I was struck specifically by how children in different cultures are integral members of their households, who were given responsibilities beyond the typical chores or homework that is the norm here in the U.S. Children in different cultures were being trained for business, responsible for the care of their older family members, and younger siblings. They frequently helped shoulder the load and were abreast of political and social matters, and, shockingly, even trained for battle at incredibly young ages. We have all seen the images of children as young as seven or eight years old, holding weapons to defend their freedoms, fighting for what they believed in, and protecting the lives of their families and communities. It's a strong example, but seeing these images did cause me to think of the world my children would one day live in--that the children from other regions of the world would one day be my children's contemporaries. It weighed heavily on my mind and influenced my belief that my children also needed to be armed. Not with semi-automatic weapons or grenades, but with spiritual gifts, knowing their purpose, the anointing of God and a resolve to stand ready to oppose any enemy at any time. Knowing there were children in the world who were living much different realities while children here in the U.S. were cluelessly watching cartoons, playing video games, and going to amusement parks challenged me to make additional adjustments to my approach to parenting, and to not get caught up in the hype. As a prophetic parent, consulting and considering scripture is pivotal prior to making parenting decisions. How does scripture record that God dealt with children?

One evening, as recorded in I Samuel 3:2-10, God calls Samuel to the ministry of prophet,

> *One night Eli, whose eyes were becoming so weak that he could barely see, was lying down in his usual place. The lamp of God had not yet gone out, and Samuel was lying down in the house of the Lord, where the ark of God was. Then the Lord called Samuel. Samuel answered, "Here I am." And he ran to Eli and said, "Here I am; you called me." But Eli said, "I did not call; go back and lie down." So he went and lay down. Again the Lord called, "Samuel!" And Samuel got up and went to Eli and said, "Here I am; you called me." "My son," Eli said, "I did not call; go back*

and lie down." Now Samuel did not yet know the Lord: The word of the Lord had not yet been revealed to him. A third time the Lord called, "Samuel!" And Samuel got up and went to Eli and said, "Here I am; you called me." Then Eli realized that the Lord was calling the boy. So Eli told Samuel, "Go and lie down, and if he calls you, say, 'Speak, Lord, for your servant is listening.'" So Samuel went and lay down in his place. The Lord came and stood there, calling as at the other times, "Samuel! Samuel!" Then Samuel said, "Speak, for your servant is listening." (NIV)

Samuel was just twelve years old. He came from a long line of Levitical priests and would go on to serve as both judge and prophet of Israel. Samuel was instrumental in facilitating the transition between Israel being governed by judges and being ruled by kings, He anointed Saul as king of Israel, then anointed David as king of Israel once Saul had been rejected from being king, and served as the messenger to speak to both kings regarding the heart of God. Another interesting fact about Samuel, and that is that like Samson, Samuel was also a Nazarite from birth.

The shepherd boy David was the youngest of his father Jesse's eight sons. He was too young to go to battle with his brothers, so he served the family as a shepherd who kept watch over the family's flock. David was a worshiper and songwriter. Many of the songs we sing today were written by David. When King Saul was rejected from serving as king of Israel, God sent Samuel to Jesse's house to anoint the next king of Israel. When Samuel arrived at Jesse's house, seven of Jesse's sons presented themselves to Samuel to be considered for the soon-to-be job opening as king. However, after looking them over, none of them fit the bill prompting Samuel to ask Jesse if these were all the sons he had. I Samuel 16:1-3,

> *"Fill your horn with oil and be on your way; I am sending you to Jesse of Bethlehem. I have chosen one of his sons to be king." But Samuel said, "How can I go? If Saul hears about it, he will kill me." The Lord said, "Take a heifer with you and say, 'I have come to sacrifice to the Lord.' Invite Jesse to the sacrifice, and I will show you what to do. You are to anoint for me the one I indicate."* (NIV)

So Samuel goes, meets up with Jesse, and begins the process of anointing one of Jesse's sons as king.

The first son had the appearance of being the right choice but God rejected him saying in I Samuel 16:7,

> *"Do not consider his appearance or his height, for I have rejected him. The Lord does not look at the things people look at. People look at the outward appearance, but the Lord looks at the heart."* (NIV)

This is such a powerful statement! That day, Jesse would parade all seven of his sons before Samuel who were of the appropriate age to serve as king, but God rejected each one of them leaving Samuel to ask if Jesse had any more sons. I Samuel 16:11-13,

> *"There is still the youngest," Jesse answered. "He is tending the sheep." Samuel said, "Send for him; we will not sit down until he arrives." Then the Lord said, "Rise and*

anoint him; this is the one." So Samuel took the horn of oil and anointed him in the presence of his brothers, and from that day on the Spirit of the Lord came powerfully upon David. Samuel then went to Ramah." (NIV)

David was around fifteen years of age when Samuel anointed him king. Although David did not take the throne immediately, soon after being anointed king is when he showed up on the battlefield and killed the giant Goliath with a slingshot and one of five smooth stones. David would go on to reign as king of Israel thirty-three years and another seven years over Hebron.

Josiah became king of Israel at the tender age of eight years old. Josiah's father and grandfather also had reigned as kings of Israel and did what was wicked and unrighteous. Although Josiah was young, he was surrendered by godly advisors who gave him wise counsel and as a result, Josiah strove to turn the people back to worshiping God. When he was about twenty years old, he began taking measures to remove idols from the land. Several years later Josiah ordered the cleansing of the temple and he called for the people to repent.

Jeremiah was a contemporary of Josiah. In chapter 1, verses, 4-8, of the book of Jeremiah, we discover a conversation Jeremiah describes between he and God when God informs him that he had been called as a prophet to the nations. "The Lord spoke His word to me, saying: "Before I made you in your mother's womb, I chose you. Before you were born, I set you apart for a special work. I appointed you as a prophet to the nations." Then I said, "But Lord God, I don't know how to speak. I am only a boy." But the Lord said to me, "Don't say, 'I am only a boy.' You must go everywhere I send you, and you must say everything I tell you to say. Don't be afraid of anyone, because I am with you to protect you," says the Lord." (NCV) As mentioned earlier, it is believed Jeremiah was between thirteen and seventeen when God called him into ministry.

Esther became Queen of Persia when she was fourteen years of age. Esther is famous for saying, "If I perish, let me perish. I am going to see the king." Esther and her cousin, Mordecai, persuaded her husband, Persian King Xerxes I to retract his order for the annihilation of all jews throughout the empire. The massacre had been instigated by Hamman, one of the king's trusted officials.

DANIEL, HANANIAH, MISHAEL & AZARIAH:
Daniel 1:1-7,

> *"In the third year of the reign of Jehoiakim king of Judah, Nebuchadnezzar king of Babylon came to Jerusalem and besieged it. The Lord gave Jehoiakim king of Judah into his hand, along with some of the articles of the house of God; and he brought them into the land of Shinar, to the house of his god, and brought the articles into the treasury of his god. And the [Babylonian] king told Ashpenaz, the chief of his officials, to bring in some of the sons of Israel, including some from the royal family and from the nobles, young men without blemish and handsome in appearance, skillful in all wisdom, endowed with intelligence and discernment, and quick to understand, competent to stand [in the presence of the king] and able to serve in the king's palace. He also ordered Ashpenaz to teach them the literature and language of the Chaldeans. The king assigned a daily ration for them from his finest food and from the wine which he drank. They were to be educated*

and nourished this way for three years so that at the end of that time they were [prepared] to enter the king's service. Among them from the sons of Judah were Daniel, Hananiah, Mishael, and Azariah. The commander of the officials gave them [Babylonian] names: Daniel he named Belteshazzar, Hananiah he named Shadrach, Mishael he named Meshach, and Azariah he named Abed-nego." (AMP)

These young men were handsome, educated, skilled, and anointed. Daniel is notorious for refusing to eat from the king's table and for later being thrown in a lion's den for refusing to obey King Darius' edict. Hananiah, Mishael and Azariah are well known for defying the pagan King Nebuchadnezzar's command for them to bow down in worship to the golden image shaped in the King's likeness when they heard the music play. As a result, these three Hebrew boys were thrown into a fiery furnace that had been heated to be seven times hotter than usual. The heat was so intense that those throwing the young men into the furnace fell dead. Theologians agree that these four young men could have been as young as eleven or twelve when they first arrived in Babylon, again, just kids.

I am extremely impressed by these four young men. Twelve, thirteen, and fourteen years of age being snatched from their homes and taken into captivity by a pagan, godless king, and transported to a godless, idolatress nation where the indulgences and lifestyles that violated God's boundaries and opposed God's way of doing things. These were common practices and part of their day-to-day life in Babylon. These young men are impressive because they consistently rejected the culture of Babylon and held to their God-given identities.

THE POWER OF PROPHETIC PARENTING

"So here's what I want you to do, God helping you: Take your everyday, ordinary life—your sleeping, eating, going-to-work, and walking-around life—and place it before God as an offering. Embracing what God does for you is the best thing you can do for him. Don't become so well-adjusted to your culture that you fit into it without even thinking. Instead, fix your attention on God. You'll be changed from the inside out. Readily recognize what he wants from you, and quickly respond to it. Unlike the culture around you, always dragging you down to its level of immaturity, God brings the best out of you, develops well-formed maturity in you."

ROMANS 12:1-2 (MSG)

In the King James Version, it reads:

"Be not conformed to this world, but be ye transformed by the renewing of your mind." Not conforming or following or falling in line with one's culture takes tremendous resolve, allegiance to God and conviction. The Prophetic Parent style is geared to produce in such a way to help their children to demonstrate such resolve, integrity and faithfulness to God and God's way of doing things in the midst of a culture that is depraved, godless, perverse and wicked.

ROMANS 12:1-2 (KJV)

I had the desire to raise children who, like the three Hebrew boys, could be in the culture, and yet possess such conviction and dedication to God that they would recognize when the culture began to lull them

They're Just Kids!

into compromising their faith. With Hananiah, Azariah and Mishael, Nebuchadnezzar went as far as to change their names to ones that honored pagan gods as soon as they were enlisted into the King's service, but their identity was not in name only. Their identities had been etched in their hearts, wills, and their consciences. Producing children who would be solid enough, secure enough, and who possessed enough godly conviction to say, "No!" when the culture attempted to woo them away from their purpose.

I recall receiving a telephone call from one of my son's coaches one evening. After saying hello, the coach immediately made the comment, "Your son intimidates me!" I was shocked and in disbelief that this forty-plus-year-old coach had telephoned me to confess that he was intimidated by my fourteen-year-old son. Of all the reasons a coach could call a parent, this was not expected. It took me a minute to wrap my mind around what the coach was saying. I asked, "What do you mean?" He repeated, "Your son intimidates me . . ." and he went on to describe how my son sits quietly on the bus as the team travels to and from basketball games across the city. He described how he and all the other players would engage in laughing, talking, joking around, and bantering back and forth with one another while my son would sit quietly reflecting and not engaging in the antics taking place around him. I thought it was so strange that a full-grown man in his forties, first of all, would admit that he was intimidated by a fourteen-year-old boy, but I also knew that my son had a certain air about himself. He had been born with it, and from a young child had literally carried himself as though he was royalty.

In that moment, I realized just how powerful parenting prophetically can be. There have been countless similar conversations with individuals over the years regarding the unique qualities and stand-out attributes of my children and as much as some parents would find occasion to gloat or boast, I know that these distinguishing characteristics are as a direct result of my parenting God's way and according to His patterns.

At age twelve, Jesus' parents found him teaching in the temple. When Mary and Joseph realized Jesus was no longer traveling beside them in route to Bethlehem, they went looking for him.

> *"Now his parents went to Jerusalem every year at the Feast of the Passover. And when he was twelve years old, they went up according to custom. And when the feast was ended, as they were returning, the boy Jesus stayed behind in Jerusalem. His parents did not know it, but supposing him to be in the group they went a day's journey, but then they began to search for him among their relatives and acquaintances, and when they did not find him, they returned to Jerusalem, searching for him. After three days they found him in the temple, sitting among the teachers, listening to them and asking them questions. And all who heard him were amazed at his understanding and his answers. And when his parents saw him, they were astonished. And his mother said to him, "Son, why have you treated us so? Behold, your father and I have been searching for you in great distress." And he said to them, "Why were you looking for me? Did you not know that I must be in my Father's house?" And they did not understand the saying that he spoke to them."*
>
> LUKE 2:41-50 (ESV)

Like all the others mentioned previously, Jesus was also just a kid. Prophetic Parenting places substantial emphasis on parents creating and maintaining an environment where children learn to hear God's voice and cultivate a meaningful relationship with Him. An environment where children are encouraged and given the liberty to flow, function and operate in their spiritual gifts and callings and in an environment where children are respected and valued as contributing members of the family. Parents, I cannot emphasize enough how important it is for your children to develop an ear to hear God's voice and the space to grow and develop into the call of God on their lives. It could mean the difference between failure and success or even life and death.

CHAPTER 11
DISMANTLING GENERATIONAL CURSES

I was challenged to reconsider including this chapter in this book. I was told that the book was valuable enough without it. After a few days of contemplation and prayer, I determined that the content of this chapter reveals one of the most significant aspects of Prophetic Parenting and I was not willing to omit it.

I was initially introduced to the concept of generational curses in the early 1990s through the television teaching ministry of Marilyn Hickey. Up until that point, I had not heard the term used. However, after listening to the teaching, and researching scripture, I recognized the validity of the existence of generational curses and how they operated, undetected, in the lives of many families.

By the early 1990s, I was well into my parenting journey prophetically. By this point, I was using every tool and technique that

I believed God had graced me with to raise my children in the way they should go. Eager to learn and grow in my effectiveness as a parent, however, led me to take a long, hard, honest look at my own life and choices along with those of my extended family as it related to generational curses. If I was able to identify the operation of generational curses within my own bloodline, having this information would be a game changer for my children.

I would be empowered with insight and information to better equip and forewarn my children of the existence of the specific, embedded spiritual landmines that they had inherited due to no fault of their own. So, I did. I took a long, hard, honest look at myself, then at my parents, at their parents, and so on. And there it was, one generation curse after another that had plagued me and my family for multiple generations! I was ecstatic and immediately began to fold this additional key component into my parenting style as I desired to give my children every possible, conceivable advantage as they grew older. Combating and conquering generational curses took my Prophetic Parenting approach to an entirely new level.

Generally, a generational curse can be described as anything that reoccurs within a family line over and over that causes harm, injury or loss. For example, alcoholism, obesity, cancer, teen pregnancy, miscarriages, suicides, murders, rage, etc. Generational curses are not hidden and can easily identified with just a little effort. Generational curses are not the same as word curses or spells spoken and conjured up by an individual against another individual. Generational curses are the result of very specific sins and iniquity perpetrated by an ancestor or distant family member.

So, when did generational curses begin? I believe it is important for parents who decide to combat generational curses as part of their prophetic parenting strategy to know what generational curses are and how they came about. When God delivered His holy people Israel from Egyptian captivity through signs, wonders and miraculous acts such as the plagues that befell Egypt and the splitting of the Red Sea, while in the wilderness, God used Moses to deliver the guidelines and regulations that would govern Israel as a holy nation. Note that Israel had been liberated and freed by God to "worship and serve" God, and become the mighty nation God had ordained them to be. In Exodus 20, the famous Ten Commandments were given and we find, for the very first time, God issued out what the consequences would be should the children of Israel disobey His regulations.

In Exodus 20:4-6 God makes this statement:

> *"You shall not make for yourself any idol, or any likeness (form, manifestation) of what is in heaven above or on the earth beneath or in the water under the earth [as an object to worship]. You shall not worship them nor serve them; for I, the Lord your God, am a jealous (impassioned) God [demanding what is rightfully and uniquely mine], visiting (avenging) the iniquity (sin, guilt) of the fathers on the children [that is, calling the children to account for the sins of their fathers], to the third and fourth generations of those who hate Me, but showing graciousness and steadfast lovingkindness to thousands [of generations] of those who love Me and keep My commandments."* (AMP)

Few of us are aware of what iniquity or idolatry might have been introduced into our ancestry three to four generations ago. Being able to pinpoint where and how a generational curse has made its way into your family is less important than identifying the existence of the curse and destroying it before it wreaks havoc in the next generation. The prophetic parent is confrontational and stands up in direct opposition to any and all spiritual snares that could potentially capsize, ambush, or upend the purpose of God coming to fruition your children's lives. Opposing and dismantling general curses is next-level parenting as it requires a keen spiritual eye and targeted focus ready to annihilate the slightest indication of a satanic plot, plan, or ploy aimed against their child. Here are the four steps to dismantling and destroying generational curses:

IDENTIFY: As I mentioned previously, generational cures are not hidden. They function and operate in plain sight, being passed from one generation to the next and can be identified quickly and easily. The simplest to identify are physical or health related. Sugar diabetes, cancer, high blood pressure, etc. Recently, Angelina Jolie underwent a "preventive" double mastectomy because she was found to carry the same ovarian and breast cancer causing gene mutation as her mother who died of ovarian cancer at age fifty-six. This deadly gene mutation had been passed from Angelina's mother to Angelina.

In my family, one of the first generational curses I identified was teen pregnancy. More specifically, I identified four generations of close relatives who had become pregnant or impregnated someone at age sixteen. It was glaring. In most cases, the pregnancy dramatically altered the trajectory of the relative's life. Professional sports opportunities disappeared, college attendance was capsized, and those pregnancies that led to teen marriages were mostly unsustainable ending in divorce. Knowledge is power. Having foreknowledge of the likely areas where your children might be vulnerable to life crippling circumstances empowers you, as the parent, to pay closer attention to those areas and to develop strategies and use techniques to gain victory in those areas. To be forewarned is to be forearmed.

ACKNOWLEDGE: As easy as it is to identify generational curses, it is not as simple acknowledging them. It has become trendy over the last couple decades for individuals and families to proclaim they are breaking generational curses, however, this is not always the case. When speaking about generational curses to other family members, you may be met with anger, outrage, offense, or even denial. It is not easy to hear or to be made aware that there is a spiritual condition resident within your family that has caused injury, harm, or loss. Whether accepted or rejected, as a parent, especially one who is parenting prophetically, it is your charge and mandate to operate in truth and transparency in this area. There is no room for you to continue to provide cover for these destructive curses. They must be acknowledged. Whether by others or not, but certainly by you. You are the one God has strategically placed within your family to come against and stand against the iniquity and idolatry that caused the generational curses in the first place. Although you may love and even respect your family, for the sake of future generations being freed from the stain and destruction caused by these ancestral curses, you must call a thing a thing.

EXPOSE: Call it out. When I first began learning about generational curses, I was humbled, honored, and thankful for the information. I'd personally experienced how these curses operated and understood that they had the potential to blindside my children if I did not make them aware. I wanted nothing more than to give my children every advantage I could so they could achieve their God given goals in life.

Making them aware of the generational curses that had toppled so many others within my family was a God send, and I was excited and grateful. However, the older generations were offended and outraged. Somehow there was the sense that I was saying our family was cursed and without fully understanding, and the family vehemently opposed my discovery. As unfortunate as this was, my commitment to my children and to my children's children far outweighed my willingness to be silent on the topic. So, every opportunity I had, I educated my children on what a generational curse was and how they had been in operation within our bloodline. I educated them on recognizing and obliterating them through awareness, prayer and spiritual warfare.

The enemy can only further his diabolical agenda under cover of darkness. When we are silent and fail to pull the covers back, this enables the enemy to continue with his dark, destructive deeds. Exposing the works of darkness by shedding light on the matter and speaking the truth concerning the state of affairs gives the enemy nowhere to run and nowhere hide. Once truth and light are introduced into the situation, the enemy can then be taken out, shut down, and defeated! Parenting prophetically is not for the timid or faint of heart. You are the truth-bearers and light-bearers for your generation and for generations to come!

OPPOSE: There are two components to opposing generational curses. The first is by denouncing them and repenting. To denounce is give official notice that a behavior or action was wrong. To repent is to view or think of an action or omission with deep regret or remorse; to ask for forgiveness and then do a 180-degree turn heading in the opposite direction. Your denunciation might be as simple as saying, "I denounce all idolatry, witchcraft, sin, and iniquity that opened portals into my family for generational curses to operate. I repent and turn away from these openings in Jesus' name." You may go further and say more as you feel directed. In either case, the important thing is that you serve notice on the enemy that it is a new day and that beginning with you and your children, generational curses will no longer have a stranglehold on our family. Through your denunciation and repentance, you are giving way to a new, blessed, favored, healed, and delivered reality for your family line for generations to come! Understand, making this stance with place you squarely in direct opposition to the enemy and there is absolutely no demilitarized zone.

The second component to opposing generational curses is through spiritual warfare. Generational curses are spiritual in nature. Whether they manifest as sickness, disease, or in other forms, at their root, they are spiritual. To destroy them, one must engage in spiritual warfare. In this spiritual battle, your greatest, most effective weapon is the word of God. God's word, scripture, is the "sword of the Spirit," as recorded in Ephesians 6:17. As a prophetic parent destroying generational curses, you will wield the sword of the Spirit, and do great damage to the kingdom of darkness. You will pray the word, teach the word, sing the word, study the word, and possibly even preach the word, but above all, if your objective is to destroy generational curses, you must live the word. Your prayers, lectures, sermons, and songs will have minimal effect if you fail to live out the word of God in your day-to-day life. It does not mean that you will always hit the mark, but your honest, humble, and sincere endeavor to strive for the mastery will translate volumes to your children. Children watch their parents and glean far more from what they see them do than what they hear their parents say. So, if breaking generational curses is your goal, the way you walk the process out will be just as important as identifying, acknowledging, and exposing the curse itself.

CHAPTER 12
LEGACY UNLEASHED: READY, AIM, FIRE!

Who would have imagined the Bible would be filled with so many densely rich nuggets and steppingstones regarding parenting effectively? This chapter explores how life looks for your child after they leave your home. Releasing and launching your children into the outside world and considering what impact your child will have on society due to how they themselves, were parented. How will your child present themselves in their day to day lives? What decisions will they make? Will they continue on the path God purposed for them? Will they deviate? Will they stray? Will they stand firm? You are not alone. These are questions and concerns most parents grapple with after their children launch. We really want to know is if our children will carry on the legacy of all we have attempted to instill and deposit in them.

For my family line, before me, there seemed to be a lack of any intentional effort to build, establish or create a legacy. Early on in my parenting years, I was exposed to a passage of scripture that states,

> *"A good man leaves an inheritance to his children's children . . ."*
>
> Proverbs 13:22 (NKJV)

The first time I heard this passage, I was shocked and amazed that such a scripture was recorded in the bible. It blew me away to realize scriptures held parents and grandparents at such a high level of accountability regarding financial or material wealth.

Legacy, on the other hand, although also passed down from one generation to future generations, represents the intangible, non-material aspects, like a person's impact on society, the memories they leave behind, or the values they instill in their descendants. I understood it to be extremely important for me to raise my children in a manner that my style of parenting would positively impact society and would live on through my posterity for generations to come. I did not want my existence on this earth as a parent to be short-lived or easily dismissed or forgotten.

It may seem incredible, but as young as I was, I understood the day would come when I would be the ancestor that future generations would either remember or have no memory of at all. Would my work and labor of love be in vain or for naught? My hope was that my children would value the journey, the lessons learned, the sacrifices and discern the magnitude of the spiritual work and investment that had gone into their rearing. I'd seen what the enemy had set up for them and through Prophetic Parenting techniques, I had been graced to create some distance between them and the diabolic plans of the adversary. But what would they do with this rich, dynamic gift?

I hoped that one day they would each pick up the baton and run with it just as passionately and fervently as I had. They would live their lives in such a way to make strategic decisions that would further distance the next generation from the plots, plans and ploys of the adversary.

I stumbled across the following passage of scripture that interestingly describes my sentiments and unspoken desires. Although I had read it numerous times throughout the years, this time I saw something new and fresh that I was prompted to share with you.

> *"Unless the Lord builds the house, its builders labor uselessly. Unless the Lord guards the city, its security forces keep watch uselessly. It is useless to get up early and to stay up late, eating the food of exhausting labor—truly He gives sleep to those He loves. Children are a gift from the Lord; a productive womb, the Lord's reward. As arrows in the hand of a warrior, so also are children born during one's youth. How blessed is the man whose quiver is full of them! He will not be ashamed as they confront their enemies at the city gate."*
>
> Psalm 127 (ISV)

In Psalm 127, the author speaks of the futility of laboring to build a family without God being the chief architect or master builder. It is what has been discussed within this book up until this point. *The Power of Prophetic Parenting* is that God is indeed recognized and enlisted as the builder and His word is the blueprint. But in the fourth and fifth verses, this Psalm unveils the legacy and the long-lasting effects of raising children with God at the helm. In verse four,

> *"As arrows in the hand of a warrior, so also are children born during one's youth."*

Arrows? Why does it correlate children with being arrows? An arrow is an offensive weapon that, when placed in a bow, stretched and aimed, has the capacity to strike, pierce and destroy its target. Prophetic parents are the warriors, and their children are the arrows in their hands. Once strategically placed, stretched, and released, your children will fly, soar, and strike targets near and far. They will soar with the wind of your parenting carrying them further than you could have ever imagined. With them, they will carry on your legacy, your training, your teachings, your mission, your ministry and your mandate! According to verse five, when enemies come to your gates, your children will deal with and destroy the enemy, and you, parent, will not be ashamed! It is your legacy, and this is God's promise to you!

When you raise your children using the Prophetic Parenting model, you are weaponizing your children against the onslaught of the enemy. Once they launch from your home, in whatever arena they find themselves, know that they will keep your memory alive, they will further the values you have instilled in them and doubtless carry on your legacy for God's glory and the advancing of His purpose.

CHAPTER 13
ESHET MANOAH

When I first started writing this book on parenting, I could hardly wait to introduce the readers to Eshet Manoah, meaning "wife of Manoah." This story affirms and proves the premise that children do indeed come with instructions, contrary to widely held beliefs. I would use her story to display and demonstrate God's care to reveal, not only the purpose of Ethet's child but also the corresponding, detailed do's and don'ts that accompanied His purpose. For months, my firm stance was to drive this point home to the reader, and in so doing, alter the course of their thinking and opening their minds to realizing they, too, had access to this detailed, instructional information regarding their own children, grandchildren, and children in their care.

But as I wrote, there was a shift in my understanding of what God purposed and intended this chapter to communicate to parents.

Soon, I began recognizing the importance of this chapter being written was not to focus on whether children come with instructions or not, but to minister life and healing to the broken hearts of multiple hundreds of thousands of parents who believed they had done everything within their power to raise their children properly only for their children to turn their backs on their upbringing and choose to travel a path contrary to the way they were raised.

I desire to begin this chapter by recognizing you, seeing you, honoring you, and acknowledging the pain of your disappointment. My prayer is that your heart will be mended and that you find peace and comfort that God has heard the cries of your heart, and changed the trajectory of this chapter specifically to affirm that you indeed have done all you knew to do to be a good parent. Not a perfect parent, because perfect parents do not exist. But certainly, a good parent.

This chapter has also been included to minister healing to the broken hearts of parents who now know they could have done so much more for their children. Parents who acknowledge they were not the best parents, and in many ways, feel as though they dropped the ball with their children. I want you to know that there is grace, forgiveness, healing, and restoration for you as well. Writing this book and penning my experiences and perspectives was intended to help, equip, and support all parents. No matter where you find yourself while reading these pages. This book is filled with love, grace, and freedom from guilt, shame and condemnation. When we know better, we do better.

Eshet Manoah's story has had a major impact on my life and on my parenting philosophy. So, I eagerly and enthusiastically included her story in this book. I became casually acquainted with Eshet Manoah and her story a little better than forty years ago. Casually because it was her son, Samson, who was the more renowned celebrity of the family and Eshet Manoah seemed to merely play an inconsequential role in the first scene of her son's fascinating and colorful life. As the years rolled on, however, and I began raising my children, my focus did shift slightly. I started to gain a little more appreciation for the role Eshet Manoah played in scripture. The scriptures state that Eshet's husband, Manoah, was a man of God and that his wife was barren. The angel of the Lord appeared to Eshet and informed her that she would conceive a child and that God uniquely chose the child to fulfill a specific purpose—the destruction of the Philistines.

> *"The angel of the Lord appeared to her and said, "You are barren and childless, but you are going to become pregnant and give birth to a son. Now see to it that you drink no wine or other fermented drink and that you do not eat anything unclean. You will become pregnant and have a son whose head is never to be touched by a razor because the boy is to be a Nazirite, dedicated to God from the womb. He will take the lead in delivering Israel from the hands of the Philistines."*
>
> JUDGES 13:3-5 (NIV)

I was so impressed by the care that was taken to communicate these details not only once to Eshet Manoah but once again for the sake of her husband, Manoah, ensuring that both parents were on the same page and understood exactly how Samson was to be raised. Because of this, her story would be one of the crown jewels of this book to demonstrate God's ability and willingness to reveal His heart regarding the purpose of a child even before the child is born. When developing the core principles of the Prophetic Parenting style, Eshet Manoah's encounter with the angel along with the details that were shared with her, impacted me deeply and shaped my approach to how I would raise my children.

As an example of the attentiveness and forethought of God as it relates to unborn children, this set of parents set significant precedence for me. If I could gain access to the heart of God regarding my children, like Eshet Manoah, I would be able to share this information with them and parent them in alignment with God's design for their lives. I felt her story would clearly demonstrate that children are born with a purpose and can actually come with instructions, contrary to what I hear society so many parents say. This one biblical account would refute the popular belief that children do not come with instructions.

Considering the environment, I can easily imagine her enthusiasm and willingness to adhere to the angel's instructions. There is no indication given to the contrary. Everything we read about this mother indicates her heart towards God and dedication to obeying God's purpose for her and her child's life. Over the months, they made preparations, and eventually Samson was born. I am pretty certain Samson was born into a family who loved and cherished him greatly, and who had high hopes and God-breathed expectations for his life.

Like many children, Samson may have felt smothered by all the fuss being made over him. He may have had a rebellious streak, being held to a higher standard than his peers. It is certainly possible, but whatever the case, Samson seemed not to have a full appreciation for how he had been raised to sanctify himself and conduct himself in life. He lived on the fringes, close to the edges, getting as dangerously close as he could to everything God had purposed him to stay away from. Samson was a fiery, complex character and his decisions were perplexing. Here was a young man who was predestined and chosen of God. Someone whose parents were given detailed instructions pertaining to his purpose and his destiny. And as you read through the account of Samson's life, he systematically violated every instruction. Samson's story is one of the saddest and most perplexing in all scripture. He had such potential. Raised in a godly, two parent home, chosen and dedicated to Good from the womb and yet, he consistently made one self-indulgent decision after another that eventually led to his demise.

From my perspective, Samson had been given every conceivable advantage to go down in history as one of the greatest judges to ever judge over Israel. Instead, Samson is most known for his lust and falling prey to the devices of his Philistine love interest, Delilah, who stripped him of everything God had given him. Samson was taken captive by the very enemy he had been anointed to destroy. His head was shaved, his eyes being gouged out, and finally coming to terms with and understanding the gravity of his God-ordained purpose, Samson finally destroyed a host of Philistines with his last fateful act of obedience.

All these years, my focus had been on the instructions and, then separately, Samson's inability to live according to and in alignment with God's purpose for his life. Not once had I considered the impact Samson's decisions must have had on his parents. While going for my morning stroll just weeks before completing this book, my heart was pierced by the brokenness and devastation Samson's parents must have experienced. Having groomed Samson for greatness and witnessing their son throw his life away. By all accounts, they had raised their children to the best of their ability. Immediately, my mind went to Eshet Manoah and I knew I must dedicate part of this chapter to the thousands of parents who have walked in their shoes. Reeling from disbelief and disappointment and suffering the anguish over losing their child in one form or another. As parents, our responsibility is to love them and train them in the way they should go, teach them, and forewarn them of the countless snares, traps, and entanglements that may lay in wait for them, but we cannot live their lives for them. As much as Eshet Manoah had dedicated her life to raising her son and wanting the best for him, there came a point when Samson's decisions were beyond her control.

As with Samson, our children will not always follow God's instructions or our desires for their lives. They will not always have an appreciation for the higher calling to which they have been called. Some children will much rather be like everyone else. The life of Samson proves this. Samson had been granted far more godly counsel than the majority of his peers. God had taken care to endow him with superhuman strength for the purpose of defeating the Philistines, along with detailed instructions on how to maintain his strength and the anointing and call of God on his life, but he would have none of it.

Parents, at the end of the day, your child does have the freedom to choose their own path, and there are no guarantees your sons or your daughters will revere God or walk in the ways of the Lord as you may desire.

Your responsibility is not to make them abide by the morals or standards you have set for them, and as heartbreaking as it may be, you must understand that ultimately, humans are free moral agents and we each have been given freedom of choice.

Scripture does not record what impact witnessing her son making one decision after another after another against God, had on Eshet Manoah. We do not know if she tried to plead with Samson or warn him of the dangerous game he was playing. We do not know if she wept, interceded, and prayed for Samson. There is no record, but as a mother, I would imagine she did.

God is with you just as He was with this couple. He sees and knows the sacrifices you have made and the love you have given. Stop beating yourself up. Do not allow guilt or shame to destroy your heart. As much as parents love their children and want the absolute best for them, there comes a point when we must truly let go and create space for God to work His perfect work in our children's lives. By every indication, they had done everything God had instructed them to do. Samson knew better! He was clear of the call of God for his life. He knew exactly what his purposes was and even shared with Delilah in great detail what God had anointed and called him to do as recorded in Judges 16:17,

> *"So he [Samson] told her [Delilah] everything. "No razor has ever been used on my head," he said, "because I have been a Nazirite dedicated to God from my mother's womb. If my head were shaved, my strength would leave me, and I would become as weak as any other man."* (AMP)

The infamous conversation between Samson and Delilah that ultimately led to Samson's greatest victory and to his death. Samson rejected God's plan, fell in love with Delilah, and in turn, Delilah sealed Samson's doom.

Once we have done our job raising them, we must then release them to walk out the rest of the journey with God as their guide. Our responsibility at that point is to pray they find their way to the path God has purposed for them.

When my children were young, I often shared Samson's story as an example of how their lives could end as someone whose affections turn away from God, falls in love with the affairs of this world, with godlessness, or who compromises their values and morals. Playing with fire will get you burned and living too close to the edge, you run the risk of falling off the other side. Make sure your children are aware that once they are out of your home, they do have choices and will have decisions to make daily on which road they will travel. As long as there is life, there is hope. Our sons and daughters are never beyond God's reach. If you have planted good seed in them, God is faithful to water that seed and cause your seed to produce much fruit.

One of the most powerful positions a parent can have is that of intercessor. To pray for and intercede on behalf of your children, over their lives and over the purpose for which God created them. As I pen the pages of this book, I stand in agreement alongside each and every one of you for the grace, favor, and goodness of God to lead, guide, and direct your sons and daughters, your grandchildren, and their children to the path of righteousness, humility, obedience, and surrender to God. I pray the anointing and power of the Holy Spirit destroy every yoke and break every chain designed and assigned to them to cause them harm, and I pray the matchless mercy and peace of God rule in your hearts and that God graces you, uplifts you, heal your heart, and removes every burden. Samson is a prime example of raising children, even with full knowledge of God's purpose for their lives and doing all you can do as a parent to follow a parenting style that produces the best outcomes. There is the possibility that your child or children will choose not to align themselves with God's design for their lives, and you have got to be ok with that. Continue to love them, pray for them and give them enough space for God to bring them back to their purpose.

CHAPTER 14
WHERE ARE THEY TODAY?

Down through the years, behavioral psychologists have studied parenting, and researchers and authors have written books to inform parents on the best ways to approach parenting. In the Power of Prophetic Parenting, I hope I have done the same. I will begin by introducing you to my four children and giving you a glimpse into the outcomes that have been wrought as a result of parenting prophetically.

THE POWER OF PROPHETIC PARENTING

My eldest, Stephen, was born at the top of the 1980's. From the moment he was born, and the nurse handed him to me, I was instantly struck to tears by the greatness that was housed within him. As a baby, toddler, and throughout his formative years, Stephen possessed a fiercely sober and vigilant demeanor. He was not easily enthralled by the frivolity of childish banter. Yes, he laughed and played and ran about like most other children, but there was always something regal about his actions that caused him to stand out and even separate himself from folly. Stephen was a "proper child." He had been marked by destiny prior to birth, and early on, I understood he was destined for greatness. Throughout his adolescence and even into his teens, Stephen walked as a god amongst mere men. No, quite the contrary. He was not arrogant, boastful, or self-indulged. Stephen was humble, benevolent, caring, and compassionate, but fierce as a lion when it came to his commitment to reaching his life's goals.

Where Are They Today?

I recognized this greatness from the first time I looked into his deep, penetrating eyes. And I was not the only one. Every school Stephen attended from grade school through college, from peers to those in authority, there were statements made pointing at the uniqueness of Stephen's character and the certainty of him having a bright, successful future. Stephen skipped first grade and, at age six fit in quite well amongst older second grade students. No matter the environment or circumstances, Stephen would inevitably rise to the occasion and then rise to the top. In 2005, He earned his bachelor's degree from UCLA in Microbiology, Immunology and Molecular Genetics. While in college, Stephen established a catering business and tutoring company that is still thriving for nearly twenty years later.

If that were not successful enough, after marriage and two children, he authored his first book, and upon learning his wife was pregnant with a set of twins a few years later, Stephen determined he was returning to school and earn another degree. In 2021, he graduated from the UCLA Anderson School of Business his FEMBA (Fully Employed Master of Business Administration). Not only did he earn this coveted degree from one of the top business schools on the planet, while working, studying and being a full-time husband and father, Stephen also became a licensed financial planner and real estate agent. For Stephen, at the plateau of every mountain, there is a higher mountain to conquer.

THE POWER OF PROPHETIC PARENTING

Roman is my second born. Born in the mid 1980's. Like Stephen, from birth, he was full of fire and self-determination. Roman, however, was far less reserved than Stephen and I quickly learned that raising him would require a completely different approach than what I'd used with Stephen. Roman was engaging, creative, inquisitive, and fearless. He never met a stranger. In fact, there were instances when in disbelief and utter horror Stephen would sound the alarm that Roman, as a toddler, was engaged in conversation with a stranger. Roman was and has always been a "people person," -- ready for the next activity or adventure. Upon his arrival, our home shifted into a stage where Rambo, Michael Jackson, and Donatello came to life and lived among us. Singing, dancing, impersonating, and doing his own stunts were just a few of the live acts Roman embodied daily. Early on Roman demonstrated his grit and grind and will to excel and master every challenge he faced.

Taking his love for entertainment to the next level, Roman attended Marymount College and majored in film. In addition to writing, he also fell in love with acting. His creative, entrepreneurial spirit led him in 2011 to write, direct, produce, and be one of the headline actors in his very first film—5 Minutes! With non- existent resources, Roman's personality, and close bonds with people affording him the ability to hold auditions, select a cast, secure locations, along with securing cameras and other film equipment, and providing craft services and a full crew including the Director of Photography (DP). If I were asked to describe Roman in one word, that word would be faith. I have been most impressed by his determination to listen for God's voice on any given matter and not move until he was certain which direction, he felt led to go. After marriage and three sons, Roman has returned to school to secure a degree in Business Finance/Accounting. For him, there is no challenge, no obstacle and no setback that has the ability to prevent him from accomplishing his dreams.

THE POWER OF PROPHETIC PARENTING

Thundering into our lives by the late 1980's was my third son, Marcus! The first three months of my pregnancy with Marcus, I threatened to miscarry on three separate occasions. I felt there was a battle raging in my womb to cut his life short and rob me of the opportunity to ever get to know him. I remember the day I cried out to God, emphatically declaring, "I want this baby!" Somehow, I felt that God would honor my decision regarding this pregnancy. From that day on, I never experienced another symptom or threat of miscarriage. Weighing a whopping 8.6 pounds and growing by leaps and bounds within his first few months, not only was Marcus huge for his age but he was equally as kind and gentle, sensitive, and loving. He was the perfect balance of both Stephen and Roman. Maybe it was just my eyes, but I assure you, with the birth of each child, I was able to see tremendous greatness shrouding, hovering, and enveloping each one, and Marcus was no different. Maybe it was God's way of giving me a glimpse into the future or of setting me up for the

Where Are They Today?

responsibility He knew what awaited me. Marcus was a gentle balance between his older two brothers. At times, quiet, reflective, observant, and at other times adventurous, 'in the mix,' and very expressive. At age three, Marcus had earned the family nickname "Walter Cronkite." With unwavering precision and absolute clarity, he meticulously reported every intricate detail of my telephone conversations. At such a tender age, how was he able to deduce and conclude what the unheard part of the conversations were?

Marcus' communication skills were just as precise. Being able to orate entire self-composed dissertations down to the smallest detail. His attention to details and facts, truths, and falsehoods, coupled with a strong dose of conviction for right and wrong led Marcus down a road of confronting and opposing discrepancies, a gift I was certain the legal field would benefit from. Marcus always had the benefit of being third in birth order. He enjoyed the privilege of rarely encountering new experiences without being flanked by his older brothers, one on his left and the other on his right and he learned from them. He taught himself to tie his shoes by watching his brothers. The same was true with his multiplication table. By age five he had taught himself how to multiply by simply listening, watching, and observing. At age six, I went to enroll him in our local elementary, and I warned the school administrator that Marcus was likely best suited for the second grade as he was advanced academically. I recall the office staff and administrator looking at me patronizingly as if to say, "All parents think their children are rock stars."

I was told to bring proof by Friday that Marcus belonged in the higher grade, but until then, he would be enrolled with his fellow six-year-old peers in first grade. I returned to the school that Friday ready to submit the requested proof only to be informed by the administrator that within his first couple of days in the first grade, he was teaching the class, so they transferred him to a second-third grade combination class. It would be a trait that would forever define who Marcus is. Following in his brother's footsteps, Marcus developed an interest in sports and by middle school, his skill level began to skyrocket. It did not hurt one bit that his height was perfect for the sport. Playing basketball in high school paved the way for him to attend and graduate from USC with his BA with an emphasis in economics. He has traveled the globe playing his sport and is also entrepreneurial, a business owner, and a father. For Marcus, there is always a simple, logical, sometimes methodical path forward, and emotions have no place in decision-making.

Where Are They Today?

Eleven years later, our family was graced with the arrival of my one and only daughter, Zion. Months before she was born, I began receiving divine impressions regarding her and what a precious gift she was and would be to me. Zion was and is the embodiment of God's favor and faithfulness to His promises. Roughly a decade before conceiving her, I'd petitioned the Lord for a daughter. As an act of faith, I purchased a box of new-born diapers and a few outfits. A couple months later, a co-worker inherited her newborn niece and expressed her need for baby items. I felt impressed to sow or give her the items I'd purchased in hopes of being blessed with a daughter. Many years later, after I'd forgotten about my belief and request to be blessed with a daughter, Zion was conceived and is the epitome of a promise kept, and a prayer answered. By the time Zion came along, her brothers were in their teens. They were fascinated by her and showered her with love and attention. Zion entered the world singing, dancing, and twirling.

She introduced a softer, less regimented dynamic to our male dominated family. Zion spent her formative years under the shadow of her high achieving and overachieving, larger than life older brothers. As daunting and overshadowing as her birth order and family dynamic was and is, she slowly but surely began finding her voice and consistently, in her own unique way, found a way to let her brilliance shine through and illuminate the lives of all who meet her. Zion spent several years singing with a children's and youth ensemble. She learned to row and eventually became president of the UNLV (University of Nevada Las Vegas) Row Crew. Zion is also a writer and recently landed her dream job as a publisher's assistant. I could not be prouder of the young lady she has become.

As you read these vivid introductions and familiarize yourself with my children, their accomplishments and their success, your mind's eye may have formed a number of different conclusions. Assumptions possibly considering that, to some degree, my children enjoyed some level of privilege or were raised in an environment that met some standard of traditional normalcy. Well, each of these assumptions would be surprisingly inaccurate.

ACKNOWLEDGMENTS

I am immensely grateful to **Willa Robinson** for her unwavering faith and obedience in hearing God's voice. Her publishing company KP Publishing, with its full weight and support, played a pivotal role in bringing this book to fruition. Willa, your dedication, grace, and steadfast support guided me through some of the darkest days when I was unable to see a light at the end of the tunnel. Your belief in this project and your commitment to its message have been truly inspiring.

I would also like to acknowledge **Pastor Ted Oden**, **Joanne Russell**, and my daughters-in-love **Noemy**, **Zuleyma**, and **Marley**, who consistently expressed the profound need for this book to be written and shared with the world. Your encouragement and belief in the importance of this work were instrumental in its creation.

To my team of intercessors, **Verleen Baker**, **Carol Fort**, **Tiffany German**, and **Ora Smith**, I extend my deepest gratitude. Your effectual, fervent prayers covered me and lifted me through the seasons of spiritual warfare that persistently attempted to halt the progress of this book. Your faith and intercession carried me through, resulting in the birth of this powerful book. Countless families will be blessed as a direct result of your willingness to pray.

With heartfelt appreciation,
Crissina D. Johnson

ABOUT THE AUTHOR

CRISSINA D JOHNSON is a highly respected family advocate, community, leader, transformational coach, and author, with more than 45 years of experience, serving in pastoral ministry and education. Throughout the past four decades, Crissina Johnson has dedicated herself to designing and developing the Prophetic Parenting Style that helps parents raise successful, confident, and resilient children. Her journey as a mother of four children and her unwavering determination has allowed her to witness extraordinary, firsthand results.

Crissina D. Johnson, a native of Southern California, embodies wisdom and insight cultivated over 45 years in pastoral ministry, education, and family advocacy. As a dedicated mother of four and grandmother of eight, she embarked on a transformative journey, pioneering the Prophetic Parenting Style to empower parents in nurturing successful, confident, and resilient children.

From an early age, Crissina's intellectual brilliance, evidenced by her exceptional IQ of 137 propelled her through a diverse academic journey, majoring in Biology, English, and Religious Studies. Simultaneously, her heart was captivated by the arts, especially drama, a passion she had honed for 14 years. This early immersion in human emotions enhanced her poise and skills as a compelling orator and storyteller.

Crissina's educational odyssey has led her through esteemed institutions such as California State University Northridge, El Camino College, Southwest College, and the University of Southern California Center for Religion Civic Culture. Along this path, she emerged as a revered community organizer, establishing POWWOW (Parents of Westchester with Orville Wright) and leaving an enduring mark on LAUSD and school sight governance committees. Her ability to unify diverse groups, coupled with her eloquence, established her as a transformative presence.

In addition to her community impact, Crissina authored *The Father's Call to Intimacy*, a profound exploration of fostering deep spiritual connections. She is the co-owner, founder, and COO of Del and Del International, a Transformational Coaching and Seminar Company. With certification as a Professional Supervised Visitation Monitor, she provides secure environments for families in transition.

In her personal life, Crissina finds fulfillment as a devoted mother and grandmother, embodying the core values she imparts in her literary works. *The Power of Prophetic Parenting* beckons readers into a transformative journey, where parenting becomes a beacon of hope, enlightenment, and enduring love for generations to come.

REFERENCES

Baumrind, D. (1966). Effects of Authoritative Parental Control on Child Behavior. Child Development, 37(4), 887–907.

Baumrind, D. (1971). Current Patterns of Parental Authority. Developmental Psychology, 4(1), 1–103.

Chao, R. K. (1994). Beyond parental control and authoritarian parenting style: Understanding Chinese parenting through the cultural notion of training. Child Development, 65(4), 1111–1119.

Chua, A. (2011). The Battle Hymn of the Tiger Mother. Penguin Books.

Dewar, G. (2011-2019). Traditional Chinese Parenting: What Research Says About Children and Why They Succeed. Parenting

Science. Retrieved from https://parentingscience.com/chinese-parenting/.

Magic Labs Media & Meridian Hill Pictures (Executive Producers). EMPIRE. Kramer, B. (Director). Kramer, L. (Producer). (2020). The Messy Truth with Van Jones and Buster Rhymes [Video file transcribed by Crissina Johnson]. Retrieved from https://youtu.be/nmswkrdzFds?si=QBEaCkXwe52DGCnKff.

Milbrand, L. (2019, July 10). Article Title: How 4 Different Parenting Styles Can Affect Your Kids. The BUMP https://www.thebump.com/a/parenting-styles#.

Taylor, M. G. (2021, November 4). Different Types of Parenting Styles. Verywell Family. Medically Reviewed by Kyle Monk, M.D. WhatToExpect. Retrieved from https://www.whattoexpect.com/family/parenting-styles/.

www.ingramcontent.com/pod-product-compliance
Lightning Source LLC
Chambersburg PA
CBHW062058290426
44110CB00022B/2635